On This Rock

ON THIS ROCK

A Call to Center the Christian Response
to Child Abuse on the Life and Words of Jesus

Victor I. Vieth

Foreword by Boz Tchividjian

Introduction by Winston D. Persaud

WIPF & STOCK · Eugene, Oregon

In memory of the children who have died from abuse, in prayer for the children living in abusive or neglectful environments, in honor of child and adult survivors everywhere, and in gratitude for the child protection professionals and other brave souls striving to care for the least of these.

Contents

Foreword

BOZ TCHIVIDJIAN[1]

Let the children come to me and do not stop them,
because the Kingdom of heaven belongs to such as these.

—MATTHEW 19:14

AS A CHRISTIAN, I celebrate the fact that Jesus was the greatest child advocate that ever walked on this earth. The God of the universe became one of us, walked among us, and lived life with us. His words matter. I can think of no one of whom Jesus spoke more highly of than children. Not only did he claim that the kingdom of heaven belongs to children, but he spoke about how children reflect God when he stated, "Whoever welcomes in my name one such child as this, welcomes me." Jesus is telling a crowd of adults that their view and treatment of children demonstrates their view and treatment of God. Wow! These are profound words spoken at a time when children were valued just a little more than slaves.

1. Boz Tchividjian is a former child abuse chief prosecutor and is the founder and executive director of GRACE (Godly Response to Abuse in the Christian Environment). He is also a law professor, and is a published author who speaks extensively on issues related to abuse within the faith community. Tchividjian is the third-eldest grandchild of Billy Graham.

Jesus's words and life tell about a God who loves, cherishes, and highly esteems little ones.

One of the greatest tragedies of the church has been how we have gradually lost sight of those precious words spoken by God with us. Instead of welcoming children, we say that they are to be "seen and not heard." Instead of celebrating the fact that children are a reflection of Jesus today, we talk about them as "being the church of tomorrow." Instead of being their greatest advocates and protectors, scores of children throughout generations have been wounded by those who profess Jesus. Instead of comforting wounded little ones, we have all too often chosen to ignore their cries. Tragically, I think we have largely forgotten Jesus's words and life when it comes to children. What does all this disheartening information have to do with Victor Vieth? I can't wait to tell you . . .

Years ago when I was a young prosecutor, God moved my heart to focus my efforts on prosecuting child sexual abuse offenses. I could not fathom a more heinous and destructive offense than the sexual abuse of a child. I have sat across from many children who have shared with me the horror and confusion of being victimized by those they loved and trusted who were supposed to protect them. This indescribable evil and devastating betrayal creates deep wounds and a lifetime of painful consequences on victims and their loved ones. One of the most troubling aspects of prosecuting these cases was that, time and time again, I witnessed churches fail to protect children and fail to advocate for those who had been abused. It seemed as though the only time church members came to court in these cases was to express support for the alleged offender. All too often, the child victim and their family were ignored, ostracized, or sometimes even vilified by the church community. This never made sense to me knowing what I know about Jesus and his high view of children and damning view of those who hurt them. Those who professed to follow Jesus displayed ugly, anti-Jesus responses and inflicted overwhelming emotional and spiritual damage upon so many abuse victims. As a Christian, I loved the church, but I became increasingly bothered and even despondent about this dark dynamic I was witnessing.

Sadly, most of my fellow prosecutors did not seem to share my concerns since many had little to no faith in Jesus, let alone his church. Then I met Victor.

I'll never forget the day. I was attending a prosecutor's training conference on child sexual offenses and saw a tall thin guy who looked like a lost high school student (and a bit like Doogie Howser, MD) standing in front of the room. To my amazement (and shock) this "high school student" was introduced as the featured speaker, Victor Vieth. For the next hour, he mesmerized me with unparalleled knowledge and passion for protecting children and prosecuting those who hurt them. I recall introducing myself to Victor afterward and walking away thinking "there is something different about that guy." In the coming months, I learned that Victor's love for Jesus fueled his passion and commitment to this difficult subject. Finally, I could recognize a follower of the One who loves, protects, and cherishes little ones. A few months later, I received a call from Victor inviting me to participate in a round-table discussion with a variety of faith leaders. The purpose was to find ways of working together for the common good by protecting children from maltreatment. During that visit, Victor Vieth became more than an expert, trainer, and conference speaker to me. He became my friend.

In the early 2000s, when I was putting together an organization to address abuse issues inside the church, Victor was one of the first people I contacted. Not only did he immediately embrace the vision and offer to be on the board, his wife Lisa (she's even cooler than Victor), suggested that we call the organization GRACE—Godly Response to Abuse in the Christian Environment. For the past fifteen years, Victor Vieth has been my advisor, confidante, teacher, colleague, and dear friend. He has walked alongside me into the dark places of the church. In those difficult, soul-wrenching moments, this saint has been an indescribable source of inspiration, encouragement, and strength. Victor Vieth has often been a much-needed reflection of Jesus into my life.

I am deeply grateful to Victor for helping me better grasp this precious truth: at the heart of the gospel is a God who is the ultimate child advocate. Jesus changed the course of history by championing children's inherent value. Victor's purpose for getting up each morning is to protect children because this is what Jesus did. Victor expends himself to exhaustion day in and day out, but his hope remains steadfast in Jesus. This hope has inspired me for almost twenty years.

I was overjoyed the day Victor informed me that he was writing a book on Jesus's life and words as a call to action for his bride to champion and protect children once again. In many ways, this book is a culmination of Victor's amazing life and all God has taught him. It is my prayer that Christians will read and listen to these profoundly important words written by this modern-day hero. However, we cannot allow ourselves to be satisfied with just listening. Our listening must propel us into action that transforms the church into a community that better reflects the love, beauty, and hope of Jesus to the least of these, because as Jesus said, the least are the greatest in God's eyes.

The theologian Henri Nouwen once wrote,

> Though they do not deny the darkness, they choose not to live in it. They claim that the light that shines in the darkness can be trusted more than the darkness itself and that a little bit of light can dispel a lot of darkness. They point each other to flashes of light here and there, and remind each other that they reveal the hidden but real presence of God.[2]

Victor Vieth is a flash of light in my life, constantly revealing the very real presence of a God who will never be overcome by darkness. That assurance and hope is what inspires me forward each day. Such a God gives me great hope that one day the darkness of abuse will be no more, and we will thank him for raising up Victor Vieth for such a time as this.

---

2. Nouwen, *The Return of the Prodigal Son: A Homecoming* (Later Printing ed., Continuum, 1996).

Acknowledgments

THIS BOOK WAS ORIGINALLY submitted as a paper for my master of arts thesis at Wartburg Theological Seminary. I'm grateful to my seminary professors Winston Persaud and Troy Troftgruben for their thorough reading and vigorous critique of early drafts of this manuscript. I'm also grateful for their encouragement to publish this work as a book in order to make it accessible to a larger audience both in and outside the church. The manuscript was also reviewed by Professor Mike Smith of Bethany Lutheran Theological Seminary, Professor John Schuetze of Wisconsin Lutheran Seminary, and Deaconess Kim Schave of the Lutheran Church Missouri Synod. Each of these reviewers provided a number of comments and suggestions that were incorporated into the final draft. Pastors Mike Sloan and Benjamin Sadler helped me in shaping the recommendations for clergy and other frontline church workers. Chris Anderson, the former executive director of Male Survivor, provided critical insights from the perspective of survivors of child maltreatment. My friend Boz Tchividjian, the founder and executive director of GRACE (Godly Response to Abuse in the Christian Environment), provided a number of thoughtful recommendations and allowed me to "test" the tenets of the book before an audience of Christian lawyers and students at his law school. Lastly, I'm grateful to my family. My father and mother, Donald and Lillian, witnessed their Christian faith by raising their two boys with gentleness. My older brother, Don, always looked out for me and helped me navigate the awkward years of childhood. My wife, Lisa, and my children, Naomi and Christian, have made enormous sacrifices to enable my work across the country, even around the world, these past thirty years. Although my children are now grown, my wife continues to encourage me in my labors even though it often means living in an empty house and making dinner for one. Everything I've accomplished, all that I am, is because of the love and support of my family.

Introduction

Rev. Winston D. Persaud, PhD[1]

THE REALITY OF CHILD abuse across the world and across the centuries is indisputable. The need to address it today is acute. That both the religious and nonreligious, as individuals and communities, are culpable is common knowledge. In Victor Vieth's book, *On This Rock: A Call to Center the Christian Response to Child Abuse on the Life and Words of Jesus*,[2] we have a timely, constructive theological challenge to the Christian community worldwide. Vieth challenges the church to return to Jesus' ineradicable declaration in the Gospel of Mark, "Taking the child in his arms, he said to them, 'Whoever welcomes one of these little children in my name welcomes me; and whoever welcomes me does not welcome me but the one who sent me'" (Mark 9:36–37). As the author's title indicates, Jesus' declaration—indeed, command—is the "rock" on which Christian response to child abuse is to be built. Vieth uses the Lutheran-confessional Law-Gospel dialectic to develop his

1. Winston D. Persaud is a professor of systematic theology at Wartburg Theological Seminary in Dubuque, Iowa. He also serves as director of the Center for Global Theologies, and is the holder of the Kent S. Knutson & United Evangelical Lutheran Church Chair in Theology and Mission.

2. This book was originally presented by Victor Vieth as an MA thesis to the faculty of Wartburg Theological Seminary and was accepted with high honors.

argument. The reader is encouraged to keep in mind this theological principle which grounds the author's appeal to the Christian community—as both judgment on its culpability and exhortation on account of the freedom in Christ—to address with thoroughness and persistence the sin of child abuse.

In order to build the case that child abuse is not a peripheral, contemporary phenomenon, which affects a tiny demographic, but that its history reaches back into the biblical times (and even before), Vieth provides a helpful summary of the history of child abuse that includes the Greco-Roman world, the Jewish community at the time of the New Testament, and the contemporary world at the time of Christ. This summary is placed alongside critical points in the findings of several studies, including the pioneering Adverse Childhood Experience (ACE) research conducted by Vincent J. Felitti and Robert F. Anda. Taken together, those studies offer a credible and insightful substantiation of the deep-seated, multifaceted damage done to victims of child abuse.

Vieth develops further the theological framework for his argument by calling attention to the incarnation's positive, liberating impact on the way children have been treated. Jesus' healthy, respectful, saving way of interacting with children, who have a prominent role in Jesus' teachings and actions, is unmistakably and definitively countercultural. Thus, whenever the individual Christian, or a group of Christians, or the church ignores, denigrates, and even rejects Jesus' incarnational way vis-à-vis children, God's judgment is inevitable. Through critical engagement of select scholarly work on the witness of the New Testament to Jesus' definitive ministry, Vieth rightly calls attention to Jesus' words of judgement on those who abuse, harm, and neglect children. In addition, references are made to vital statements in both Luther's writings and the Lutheran Confessions which heighten and illumine the thrust of the biblical witness.

Vieth provides an honest, sobering summary of the welcome, liberating responses of the early church to child abuse, on the one hand, and the shameful ways in which the church departed from Jesus' "way" with children, on the other hand. This departure shows a history of the church as culpable in contributing to the physical and sexual abuse of children, and their neglect. Using the sharpness of his training and experience as a lawyer, Vieth draws attention to the emerging awareness, in both church and wider society, of credible reports on child abuse in churches. In addition, Vieth points to the acute need for further work in the legal system and its implications for the church to broaden and deepen its effectiveness in responding to child abuse. Of course, the author makes a particular appeal to the Christians and the church to let their lives and ministry reflect the biblical witness.

Vieth concludes his argument with an articulation of "ten commandments" whose implementation he sees would improve the state of children and significantly, even radically, stem the powerful, damaging tide of child abuse. Attending to these commandments, even just one or a few, the author is convinced, would be salutary. Such attention, normed by Jesus' teaching and actions, which judges the silence of Christians and the church to child abuse and/or their inadequate response, would instantiate Jesus' promise that he is thereby welcomed.

With this brief introduction to this much-needed work, the reader is invited to read, ponder, and, in concrete, practical ways, engage the argument in church and society.

1

Welcoming Children
as Christ's Messengers

Taking the child in his arms, he said to them,
"Whoever welcomes one of these little children in my name welcomes
me; and whoever welcomes me does not welcome me but the one who
sent me."

—MARK 9:36–37[1]

THE IMAGE OF JESUS shielding a child in his arms and tenderly
uttering the admonition to welcome children as we would welcome God (Mark 9:36–37) is the subject of artwork and children's
music, but its radical pronouncement is seldom made clear in the
Christian church. Indeed, theologians often expand the plethora
of Christ's words about children or "little ones" as broad references
to the poor or the suffering who respond to the gospel.[2]

---

1. Unless noted otherwise, all scriptural references are taken from the
NRSV.

2. Strange, *Children in the Early Church*, 55.

In the text from Mark's Gospel, though, Christ's words are unmistakable. Jesus is referencing ancient Jewish customs involving messengers. Given the distances over which communications had to be brought, the bearers of news were to be treated with great respect—a respect equal to that accorded the person sending the message.[3] Through this analogy, Jesus is contending we should receive a child as Christ's "chosen representatives."[4] Stated differently, our treatment of children says everything about how we regard Jesus and, since Christians regard Jesus as God,[5] our treatment of children reflects our attitude toward our Creator.

If this is true, and many scholars are confident it is,[6] then it is critical to examine the response of the Christian community to children. Nowhere is this more important than the response of Christians to abused and neglected boys and girls. To this end, this book will examine the prevalence and impact of child maltreatment through the lens of Christian obligations. Accordingly, we will review what is known about child abuse today as well as at the

3. Strange, *Children in the Early Church*, 54.

4. Strange, *Children in the Early Church*, 54.

5. In the second article of the Apostles' Creed, Christians confess to believe in "Jesus Christ, his only Son, our Lord" who rose from the dead, is "seated at the right hand of God" and will return to "judge the living and the dead." In his explanation of the second article, Martin Luther asserts a Christian believes that Jesus Christ, "true God, begotten of the Father from eternity, and also a true human being, born of the Virgin Mary, is my Lord. He has redeemed me, a lost and condemned human being. He has purchased and freed me from all sins, from death, and from the power of the devil, not with gold or silver but with his holy, precious blood and with his innocent suffering and death. He has done all this in order that I may belong to him, live under him in his kingdom, and serve him in eternal righteousness, innocence, and blessedness, just as he is risen from the dead and lives and rules eternally." Luther, "Small Catechism," in Kolb and Wengert, *Book of Concord*, 355.

6. Commenting on this text, one scholar notes that according a guest honor is to serve him or her. Accordingly, a true disciple of Christ must "love and serve children." Gundry-Volf, "The Least and the Greatest," 43. Commenting on the parallel text in the Gospel of Luke, another scholar calls children "Jesus' own envoy" and notes that whoever honors the child honors Jesus and, in turn "honors God." Carroll, "What Then Will This Child Become?," 177, 189.

time of Christ and then explore the life and teachings of Jesus as they pertain to maltreated children.

As evidenced by a number of child abuse scandals in the Christian community, it is clear that the contemporary church has often failed to adhere to the words of Christ. Even worse, our teachings and conduct have sometimes contributed to the abuse and neglect of children. It was not always this way. Although far from perfect, there is evidence many early Christians took seriously the words of Jesus toward children and often distinguished themselves as strong voices for protecting children from all forms of abuse.

In light of Christ's teachings and Christian history, this book proposes the church not do anything new but rather something very old. Specifically, we need to return to the message of Jesus and center our responses to child abuse on the words and actions of Christ. With this focus in mind, the book envisions a very different church going forward—a church firmly rooted in and fully committed to Christ's teachings on children.

In advancing this argument, two underlying propositions must be kept in the forefront. First, and most importantly, Jesus is not a mere mortal but rather the Word incarnate (Augsburg Confession, BC 39:1).[7] As expressed in the Holy Scriptures and the Lutheran Confessions, Jesus is both "true God" and "true human being" (Augsburg Confession, BC 39:1; 355:4). As true God, Jesus has "immeasurable power, wisdom, and goodness" (Augsburg Confession, BC 37:2). Accordingly, Jesus' teachings pertaining to child abuse and neglect should not be regarded lightly or as optional for the Christian. If we reject Jesus' teachings on this or other subjects, we are rejecting the wisdom and goodness of the eternal Word of God through whom the universe was created (John 1:1–3a).

---

7. In this paper, all references to "BC" are to the Book of Concord. The first numerals in the text are to the page number and the second is to the numbered section on that page. Accordingly, BC 39:1 directs the reader to the 39th page of the book of concord, section 1. Kolb and Wengert, eds., "Augsburg Confession," in *Book of Concord*, 39.

Second, in contending the Christian community has repeatedly ignored, even willfully refused to adhere to the teachings of Jesus on the maltreatment of children, this book applies the biblical principle of law and gospel (Formula of Concord, BC 500:1). In contrasting the words of Jesus with the actions of his followers, this book directs Christians to their sins in the hope of genuine repentance. It is through faith that God's grace and the forgiveness of our sins is apprehended (Augsburg Confession, BC 57:27). If this happens, the Holy Spirit will provide hearts "renewed and endowed with new affections" toward God (Augsburg Confession, BC 57:29) and, in turn, the children Jesus has directed us to protect.

2

Like a Footprint in Wet Cement

The Prevalence and Impact of Child Abuse in the Modern Era

THE PHYSICAL AND EMOTIONAL IMPACT OF CHILD ABUSE

IN 1998, DR. VINCENT Felitti was overseeing a major weight loss control program when he noticed something shocking—the patients who were the most successful in losing weight were also the quickest to drop out of the program and rapidly regain the weight. In fact, they would regain their weight at a level Felitti previously thought was physiologically impossible.

As it turns out, these patients had endured various forms of childhood trauma, or "adverse childhood experiences" (ACEs) such as physical, sexual, or emotional abuse. These patients ate excessively as an unconscious or conscious coping mechanism. To these patients, overeating was a solution to "problems dating back to the earliest years, but hidden by time, by shame, by secrecy."[1]

---

1. Felitti and Anda, "Relationship of Adverse Childhood Experiences," 77.

Having found a correlation between obesity and child abuse, Felitti and his team of researchers contemplated the possibility that other medical and mental health conditions could be related to abuse. To this end, they queried over 17,000 adult patients to determine if they had endured one or more of ten adverse childhood experiences.[2]

What Felitti found was a massive level of trauma across the population. More than one out of four patients had been beaten as children. More than one out of four women and nearly one out of six men were sexually abused. Thirteen percent witnessed domestic violence, and 10 percent had food, clothing, shelter, or other necessities withheld from them during childhood. More than one out of ten were called stupid and ugly or otherwise humiliated with words that hurt.

A patient who fit into one category, such as physical abuse, received an ACE score of 1. This is true no matter how many times the patient was physically abused. In other words, a patient who was beaten one time and a patient who was beaten fifty times both received an ACE score of 1. If, though, the patient fit into a second category such as sexual abuse, they now received an ACE score of 2. If they fit into a third category, such as emotional abuse, the ACE score became 3 and so on. Accordingly, a patient could have an ACE score ranging from 0 (no adverse childhood experiences)

2. The ten categories of adverse childhood experiences and the percentage of patients having endured each experience is as follows:
- Emotional abuse (humiliation, threats)—(11%)
- Physical abuse (beating, not spanking)—(28%)
- Contact sexual abuse (28% women—16% men)
- Mother treated violently (13%)
- Household member alcoholic or drug user (27%)
- Household member imprisoned (6%)
- Household member chronically depressed, suicidal, mentally ill, psychiatric hospitalization (17%)
- Not raised by both biological parents (23%)
- Neglect—physical (10%)
- Neglect—emotional (15%), see 78–79.

to 10 (meaning the patient had adverse experiences fitting into all ten categories).

If a patient simply had an ACE score of 1 they were nonetheless more likely to suffer from numerous medical and mental health conditions including:

- Cancer
- Heart disease
- Sexually transmitted diseases
- Liver disease
- Smoking
- Alcohol abuse
- Obesity
- Drug dependence
- IV drug use
- Early intercourse, pregnancy
- Depression
- Anxiety disorders
- Hallucinations
- Sleep disturbances
- Memory disturbances
- Anger problems
- Domestic violence risk
- Job problems
- Relationship problems[3]

The risk of these and other conditions increased the higher the ACE score with patients having an ACE Score of 6 or more

---

3. Felitti and Anda, "Relationship of Adverse Childhood Experiences," 78–84.

facing "a lifespan almost two decades shorter than seen in those with an ACE score of 0 but otherwise similar characteristics."[4]

"In the context of everyday medical practice," Felitti concluded, "we came to recognize that the earliest years of infancy and childhood are not lost but, like a child's footprints in wet cement are often lifelong."[5]

THE SPIRITUAL IMPACT OF CHILD ABUSE

In a review of thirty-four studies reporting on a total of 19,090 adult survivors of child maltreatment, scholars noted that most studies found abuse damaged the faith of children, often by damaging the victim's view of and relationship with God.[6] In a study of 527 victims of child abuse (physical, sexual or emotional), researchers found these children had a significant "spiritual injury" such as feelings of guilt, anger, grief, despair, doubt, fear of death, and belief that God is unfair.[7]

When the perpetrator is a member of the clergy, the impact on the victim's spirituality is often heightened. This happens, in part, because clergy abusers often use their religion to justify or excuse their abuse of children and then communicate these cognitive distortions to their victims.[8] In one case, for example, a minister told his daughter that having sex with children is sometimes acceptable and cited God's use of incest at the time of Adam and Eve and after the flood as proof.[9] As a result of this distorted theology, the church attendance of these children decreases, they are less likely to trust God, and their relationship with God "ceases to grow."[10]

4. Felitti and Anda, "Relationship of Adverse Childhood Experiences," 84.

5. Felitti and Anda, "Relationship of Adverse Childhood Experiences," 84.

6. Walker et al., "Changes in Personal Religion/Spirituality."

7 Drebing et al., "Long Term Impact of Child Abuse," 369.

8. Vieth, "What Would Walther Do?," 257. McLaughlin, "Devastated Spirituality," 145.

9. Vieth, "Ministering to Sex Offenders," 208.

10. McLaughlin, "Devastated Spirituality," 145.

3

Attitudes toward Children in the New Testament Era

CHILDREN IN THE GRECO-ROMAN WORLD

IN THE GRECO-ROMAN WORLD, the concept of *logos*, the ability to reason, primarily determined the value of a human being.[1] Plato, Aristotle and other philosophers spoke harshly about the faculties of children and, as a result, children were "associated with stupidity" and their opinions were no more valuable than those of animals.[2] Children were disparaged for their weakness and lack of courage, with Cicero observing, "The thing itself cannot be praised, only its potential."[3] On the other hand, some scholars distinguish between the "writings of elite, citizen men" who "frequently speak of children in unflattering and dismissive ways" and the actual families who reared boys and girls.[4] Although this distinction is

---

1. Bakke, *When Children Became People*, 15.
2. Bakke, *When Children Became People*, 16–17.
3. Bakke, *When Children Became People*, 18–19.
4. Betsworth, *Children in Early Christian Narratives*, 9.

valid, the harsh societal view of children likely contributed at some level to their neglect and abuse throughout the Roman Empire.[5]

CHILDREN IN THE JEWISH COMMUNITY

In the Jewish community of the New Testament era, children were critical in sustaining an agrarian community but also continuing a covenantal relationship with God.[6] To this end, there was an emphasis on purity in marriage "and an equally strong emphasis on the careful education and upbringing of children born within the covenant."[7] The Jewish historian Josephus notes that boys were taught to read in order to "learn both the laws and the deeds of their forefathers."[8] In comparison to the wider Greco-Roman culture, the Jewish community "nurtured a higher view of infant life" and placed a greater emphasis on educating all boys.[9] Although children were considered a great blessing from God, this "did not preclude denigrating them as lacking in understanding" and in need of "strong discipline."[10]

In addition to strong discipline, Jewish children faced other hardships. It was not unusual for these children to be sold into slavery to pay a debt, and some Jewish historians contend that fathers were "frequently" forced by their creditors to sell pre-menstrual daughters.[11] With respect to child sexual abuse, the Mishnah[12] pro-

5. For example, although some scholars contend that pederasty was an "elitist pastime" which was rare in agrarian society, Christian Laes believes such arguments "smack of intellectual dishonesty" and cites evidence the sexual abuse of boys was "very present" throughout the Roman world. Laes, *Children in the Roman Empire*, 246.

6. Strange, *Children in the Early Church*, 10–11.

7. Strange, *Children in the Early Church*, 12.

8. Strange, *Children in the Early Church*, 13.

9. Strange, *Children in the Early Church*, 37.

10. Gundry, "Children in the Gospel of Mark," 143.

11. Bartchy, "Slaves and Slavery in the Roman World," 171.

12. The Mishnah represents "rabbinical interpretation and application of the laws found in the Torah." Although written in the second century CE, it "can be safely assumed" that a number of its teachings were in place at the time

hibited the rape of children, but the penalty for an adult male who sexually assaulted a child below the age of three was simply a fine, with harsher penalties reserved for sexually assaulting an adult.[13] This is the world into which Christ was born.

---

of Christ. Rueger, *Sexual Morality*, 43–44.

13. Rueger, *Sexual Morality*, 54.

4

Child Abuse at the Time of Christ

ALTHOUGH PARENTS IN THE New Testament era loved their children, there was also a "casual and almost off-hand brutality in the day-to-day treatment of the young."[1] We do not, of course, have the equivalent of an Adverse Childhood Experience (ACE) study to aid in determining the extent of this brutality. Even so, there are at least three factors that likely made child maltreatment relatively common. First, there was a widely accepted concept of "Greek love" which legitimized the sexual exploitation of boys.[2] Second, the institution of slavery enabled masters to violate children in myriad ways.[3] Third, children were generally held in low esteem.[4] These and others factors played a role in the neglect of children as well as their physical, sexual, and emotional abuse.[5]

---

1. Bakke, *When Children Became People*, 2.

2. Bakke, *When Children Became People*, 34.

3. Bakke, *When Children Became People*, 34.

4. Bakke, *When Children Became People*, 34.

5. Additional factors include poverty and a poor understanding of child development. Poverty contributed to exposure of children and the selling of them into slavery. A limited understanding of child development contributed to discipline rooted primarily in violence.

PHYSICAL ABUSE

Since children had at best a "limited measure of reason," teachers in the Greco-Roman world had a "conscious conviction" to "employ physical punishment to check children and slaves."[6] When children lost their baby teeth, usually around the age of seven, they would either go to school or learn a trade but, in either setting, beatings were deemed necessary to "develop rationality and self-control."[7] Likening children to animals, Seneca noted the necessity to "inflict suffering and punishment" on children in the way we "break in animals by using the lash."[8]

Archaeological finds from this era include depictions of two boys holding down a third child in order to make a teacher's beating easier as well as graffiti referencing physical brutality.[9] In addition to Greco-Roman schooling, Jewish education at the time also employed strict discipline of children.[10]

The physical abuse of children by their parents was "quite common,"[11] as reflected by the fact "a number of texts either assume or state explicitly that children were beaten and harshly disciplined by their parents."[12] In the Wisdom of Sirach, for example, parents are told to whip their children frequently (Sir 30:1).[13]

It's also important to note that many children were slaves. Given our general knowledge of the treatment of slaves in this era, there is a "good reason" to believe that beatings or other violence was a "constant reality" for a majority of these boys and girls.[14]

---

6. Bakke, *When Children Became People*, 21.

7. Cohick, "Women, Children and Families," 185.

8. Bakke, *When Children Became People*, 21, citing Seneca, *Constant*, 12.3.

9. Laes, *Children in the Roman Empire*, 143.

10. Yinger, "Jewish Education," 328.

11. Yinger, "Jewish Education," 328.

12. Bakke, *When Children Became People*, 40.

13. The Wisdom of Jesus Son of Sirach (also known as Ecclesiasticus) was written in the early second century BCE and was designed to "instruct people in wisdom so they may make even greater progress in living according to the Law of Moses." Engelbrecht, *Apocrypha*, 73.

14. Bakke, *When Children Became People*, 41.

As noted in the Wisdom of Sirach, wayward slaves "will not lack bruises" (Sir 23:10). In addition to acts of violence experienced at the hands of parents, teachers, or trade masters, governmental officials also exposed children to extreme acts of violence. For example, it was not "off limits" for children to view public executions and acts of torture[15] or "sadistic spectacles."[16]

NEGLECT

In the Greco-Roman world, as many as 50 percent of all children died before the age of ten[17] and 30 percent died in their first year of life.[18] The high mortality rate was attributable to unsanitary conditions, poor nourishment, and epidemics.[19] Although death was greater among the poor,[20] the mortality rate of children among the upper class was also pronounced.[21]

Given these conditions, it was "legally permissible and socially acceptable" for parents to leave children exposed to the elements where they would die or, in some instances, be taken in by others.[22] Although poverty was a primary reason children might be exposed, parents also left their children on the roadside if an infant was deemed illegitimate or if the parents received "omens of doom" that led them to fear raising the child.[23] Children born with a deformity or deemed weak were also exposed or simply drowned.[24]

---

15. Cohick, "Women, Children and Families," 185.

16. Laes, *Children in the Roman Empire*, 138.

17 Bakke, *When Children Became People*, 23.

18. Betsworth, *Children in Early Christian Narratives*, 77.

19. Bakke, *When Children Became People*, 23.

20. Cohick, "Women, Children and Families," 185.

21. Bakke, *When Children Became People*, 23.

22. Bakke, *When Children Became People*, 29.

23. Bakke, *When Children Became People*, 30.

24. Bakke, *When Children Became People*, 31.

The decision to expose a child was typically made by the father. According to Lynn Cohick:

> If the newborn seemed strong and healthy to the midwife, she would present the child to the father for acceptance or rejection. If the father embraced the newborn laid before him, the child was raised in the house; if the father rejected the child, he or she was just put out.[25]

Children who were rescued, known as "foundlings," were not necessarily adopted or otherwise cared for but often became victims of slavery or sexual exploitation.[26] It is not clear how many exposed children died and how many were "rescued," but the greater weight of historical evidence suggests a majority of the infants died.[27]

SEXUAL ABUSE

According to Lloyd deMause, children in the Greco-Roman world "lived in an atmosphere of sexual abuse," including "boy brothels," the selling of children into concubines, and the sexual abuse of children by their teachers.[28] The Roman Empire continued a Greek custom of "gymnasiums" in which it was not uncommon for adolescent boys to "wrestle" naked with their male coaches.[29] This, in turn, contributed to acts of intercourse or fondling of these children.[30] Some Romans objected to the sexual abuse of boys, contending the children received "nothing but tears and pain"—but the practice continued.[31]

25. Cohick, "Women, Children and Families," 184.

26. If the identity of the parent who exposed the child became known, even years later, it was possible for the child to be reclaimed by his or her original family, which could mean an escape from slavery. Evans Grubbs, "Hidden in Plain Sight," 306.

27. Bakke, *When Children Became People*, 32.

28. DeMause, *History of Childhood*, 43.

29. Rueger, *Sexual Morality*, 19.

30. Rueger, *Sexual Morality*, 19.

31. Rueger, *Sexual Morality*, 20.

O. M. Bakke concludes that most of the children rescued from exposure, "boys and girls alike," were sexually exploited.[32] Although it is impossible to determine the precise extent of sexual abuse, outside of freeborn children in the Roman Empire[33] "it appears that sexual relationships between children and men were socially accepted, and it is reasonable to assume they were relatively common."[34] The situation for slave children was even worse with children "sexually available to their owners" and also subjected to being prostituted.[35]

EMOTIONAL ABUSE

There is little doubt that parents in the Greco-Roman era had affection for their children and grieved their passing. Nonetheless, some scholars contend the high mortality rate and the low esteem in which young children were held caused some parents not to emotionally invest in their children.[36] There is an absence of epitaphs for deceased infants during this era, and Cicero, among others, chastised parents for grieving over dead babies, likening his own dead grandchild to "a thing."[37] If there was an emotional distance it may also be because parents were rarely the primary caregivers of their children.[38] Beyond these general observations, the best we can say is that the sources addressing the extent of emotional abuse or neglect "are open to interpretation."[39]

---

32. Bakke, *When Children Became People*, 44.

33. Violating a free Roman boy was considered a crime. Cohick, "Women, Children and Families," 185.

34. Bakke, *When Children Became People*, 44–45.

35. Cohick, "Women, Children and Families," 185.

36. Bakke, *When Children Became People*, 45.

37. Bakke, *When Children Became People*, 45.

38. Cohick, "Women, Children and Families," 185.

39. Bakke, *When Children Became People*, 46.

5

Jesus as a Child

The Impact of the Incarnation on the Treatment of Children

JESUS WAS BORN INTO a Jewish family living in the Greco-Roman era. As we have seen, there is no reason to believe the rate of child abuse was less than in our modern era and a number of reasons to believe it was likely much higher. Did the birth of Jesus, and the limited Gospel accounts of Christ's childhood, influence this culture in any way? In particular, did the concept of God becoming a baby influence societal views about children?[1]

In the Gospel of Matthew we are told that the infant Christ was conceived by the Holy Spirit and that this baby's name is Emmanuel, which means "God is with us" (Matt 1:23). Sometime later, wise men from the East traveled a great distance only to kneel

---

1. As noted by the World Council of Churches, the notion of God becoming an incarnate baby "seems strange to the modern mind" and thus the incarnation is "often replaced by modern views of Jesus as a hero, a mystic, a religious teacher and genius, a revolutionary, or a moral example." See WCC, *Confessing the One Faith*, 29. The modern view, though, is contrary to Scripture (John 1:1–3) and the creeds which teach us our faith in Jesus "is not in a human being blessed and used by God, but in the Son of God from eternity to eternity." WCC, *Confessing the One Faith*, 36.

before this child and to bestow gifts (Matt 2:1–2, 11). The enemies of this baby also recognized the actual or potential power of the child. We are told the infant was nearly the victim of infanticide at the hands of King Herod but God protected the child by warning Joseph to flee (Matt 2:13, 16).

In Matthew's Gospel, the five recorded episodes in Christ's infancy narratives all include a citation to the Hebrew Bible (Matt 1:18–25; 2:1–12, 13–15, 16–18, 19–23) which functions to establish that Christ's life, including his childhood, is part of God's will from the very beginning.[2] In other words, it was always God's intent to save the world through the birth of a child at a particular point in history.[3]

The miraculous nature of the incarnation is even clearer in the Gospel of Luke as the angel tells Mary "the child to be born" will be both holy and the very "Son of God" (Luke 1:35). Elizabeth calls Mary "the mother of my Lord" (Luke 1:43) and Mary herself suggests that her infant son is also her Savior (Luke 1:47). A heavenly choir of angels praises God on account of this birth and one of the angels tells shepherds the child is their "Savior," the long-awaited "Messiah" (Luke 2:11–14).

At the time of Jesus' circumcision, Simeon called the baby a "light for revelation to the Gentiles and for glory to your people Israel" (Luke 2:32). The prophetess Anna spoke about the child being the "redemption of Jerusalem" (Luke 2:38). Luke tells us the "favor of God" was with the child and, by the age of twelve, Jesus had temple teachers spellbound with the depth of his understanding of the scriptures (Luke 2:40, 46–47).

---

2. Betsworth, *Children in Early Christian Narratives*, 77.

3. See Eph 1:7–12 and Gal 4:4. The reference to the "fullness of time" in Eph 1:10 "provides an important nuance" because it means "God has ordered or arranged the various periods of history to implement the salvation of the world." Joersz, *Reformation Heritage Bible Commentary*, 100–101. Christian historians point to numerous factors in the Greco-Roman world "to show how the 'time was ripe' for the Savior to be born." Joersz, *Reformation Heritage Bible Commentary*, 101.

The inclusion of these birth narratives in the Gospels of Matthew and Luke had "momentous consequences."[4] Perhaps reflecting the prevailing cultural attitudes toward children, many early Christians struggled with the idea of God as a baby. As late as the fifth century, this struggle was continuing with Nestorius denying that "God is two or three months old."[5]

Once the doctrine of the incarnation took hold, and Christians realized the Creator of the universe (John 1:1–3) once nursed at his mother's breast, the human view of children necessarily changed for the better and forever. As W. A. Strange writes, "If the incarnate Christ had assumed the experiences of childhood, as well as those of adult life, then childhood itself took on a new dignity and importance."[6]

The new dignity bestowed on children through the incarnation was not simply limited to Jesus' birth. As the Eternal Word, Jesus' entire life and actions toward children elevated their status in the family, in society, and the church. The baby Jesus, the incarnate Word of God who was nearly the victim of infanticide, was destined to "rise up in defense of children."[7]

4. Strange, *Children in the Early Church*, 46.
5. Strange, *Children in the Early Church*, 46.
6. Strange, *Children in the Early Church*, 46.
7. Offit, *Bad Faith*, 126.

6

Jesus and the Children

"CONTRARY TO THE ETHOS of his time," writes Paul Offit, "Jesus didn't view children as objects; he believed that anyone who was human couldn't be alien to God, that all were part of God's kingdom" and that "Jesus' love of children is evident throughout the New Testament."[1] This conclusion can be seen when examining the prominent role of children in the ministry and teachings of Jesus, in Jesus' warnings to those who would hurt children, and his promised judgment on those who fail to care for the suffering.

In addition to the life and teachings of Jesus, the Gospel of Matthew points to another factor evidencing Christ's commitment to victims of abuse. According to Matthew, Jesus is the descendant of not one but three victims of sexual exploitation—a clear indication that God's kingdom includes the marginalized, the oppressed, and victims of abuse.

1. Offit, *Bad Faith*, 126.

SEXUAL EXPLOITATION IN THE LINEAGE OF CHRIST

In the Gospel of Matthew, readers are given a lineage of Christ (Matt 1:1–17) that consists of many of the "movers and shakers in the history of Israel."[2] There is, though, a remarkable break in this lineage—we are also told that Jesus is the descendant of five women, including three who were at some level sexually exploited: Tamar (Gen 38); Rahab (Josh 2:1; 6:22–25); and Bathsheba (2 Sam 11).[3] Indeed, the very mother of Christ faced "public disgrace" because of the nature of her pregnancy (Matt 1:19). This history nicely sets the stage for a God who consistently sides with victims—including child victims. Simply stated, it is in the Lord's blood.

THE PROMINENT ROLE OF CHILDREN IN THE MINISTRY AND TEACHINGS OF CHRIST

As a simple illustration of the prominent role of children in the ministry of Christ, consider this. In the Hebrew Bible, what Christians term the "Old Testament," the word "children" appears 16 times[4] in the 1,400-plus pages of text.[5] In contrast, the word "children" appears 25 times[6] in the 500-plus pages of the New

---

2. Betsworth, *Children in Early Christian Narratives*, 76.

3. For a discussion of the sexual assault of Tamar and the "power rape" of Bathsheba, see Davidson, "Sexual Abuse in the Old Testament," 144–50.

4. *Concordia Self-Study Bible*, concordance 16. The Hebrew Bible uses of the word "child" or "children" are found in Exod 20:5; Deut 4:9; 6:7; 11:19; 14:1; 24:16; 30:19; 32:46; Job 1:5; Ps 8:2; 78:5; Prov 17:6; 20:7; 31:28; Joel 1:3; Mal 4:6.

5. In the *Concordia Self-Study Bible*, the Hebrew Bible text consists of 1,435 pages of text.

6. *Concordia Self-Study Bible*, concordance 16. The Greek Bible uses of the word "child" or "children" are found in Matt 7:11; 11:25; 18:3; 19:14; 21:16; Mark 9:37; 10:14, 16; 13:12; Luke 10:21; 18:16; John 1:12; Acts 2:39; Rom 8:16; 1 Cor 14:20; 2 Cor 12:14; Eph 6:1, 4; Col 3:20, 21; 1 Tim 3:4, 12; 5:10; Heb 2:13; 1 John 3:1.

Testament.[7] Nearly half of these references, twelve in total, are contained in the words of Christ.[8]

Jesus' Knowledge of and Interactions with Children

In the Synoptic Gospels, it appears Jesus knew children well enough that he was aware of the games they played (Matt 11:16–18). Jesus prayed for children (Matt 19:13–14) and blessed them (Mark 10:13–16).[9] On two occasions in Mark's Gospel, we are told of Jesus taking children in his arms (9:36–37; 10:13–16), and in Luke's Gospel, even babies were the recipients of the Lord's touch (Luke 18:15–17).

Jesus' Healing of Children

The Gospels also record several instances in which Jesus not only healed a child but did so tenderly. When a man tells Jesus of a tormented son, the Lord asks, "How long has he been like this?" (Mark 9:21). After Jesus removed the demon, some thought the boy to be a corpse but Jesus took the boy by the hand and lifted him up (Mark 9:25). When raising Jairus' daughter from the dead, Jesus called the child "little girl," and reminded those gathered to give her something to eat (Mark 5:41–43). In another instance, though, Jesus tested a woman's faith by suggesting he was not called to heal the daughter of a Gentile woman—but then rewarded her persistence (Mark 7:24–29).[10]

---

7. In the *Concordia Self-Study Bible*, the Greek Bible text consists of 528 pages.

8. Matt 7:11; 11:25; 18:3; 19:14; 21:16; Mark 9:37; 10:14, 16; 13:12; Luke 10:21; 18:16; and John 1:12.

9. The reference to Jesus blessing the children is the only time the Greek verb *kateulogeo* is used in the New Testament. Paavola, *Mark*, 182.

10. "The healing is all due to Jesus' compassion and power," but the woman's persistence "express the faith and close relationship that receives His gift." Paavola, *Mark*, 133.

Jesus' Theology of the Child

In the Synoptic Gospels, Jesus uses children to make at least four theological points. First, Jesus uses children to illustrate the difference between earthly and heavenly parenting. Jesus does this through the observation that even sinful parents know to give their children fish and bread as opposed to stones and snakes (Matt 7:9–11). In making this comment, Jesus implicitly acknowledges the wrongfulness of child neglect but uses good, or at least marginally good, parenting to illustrate a greater lesson—that God gives greater gifts than even loving parents provide their children (Matt 7:11).

Second, Jesus uses children as an illustration of ideal faith. When the disciples continue to quibble as to who is the greatest in the kingdom of heaven (Matt 18:1; 20:21; Luke 22:24), Jesus puts a child in the midst of them and instructs, "Unless you change and become like children, you will never enter the kingdom of heaven" (Matt 18:2–3). Jesus goes on to say, "Whoever becomes humble like this child is the greatest in the kingdom of heaven" (Matt 18:4). Since children are humble in their dependence and trust in others, Jesus is contending that God's people are "characterized by humble trust in the Lord."[11] Then, most astonishingly, Jesus adds "Whoever welcomes one such child in my name welcomes me" (Matt 18:5).

These words of Jesus were countercultural to the religious and societal structures of the day.[12] Moreover, the words of Jesus demand, both then and now, that Christians adopt a proactive approach to addressing the physical and spiritual needs of children.[13] Although sinful mortals can never completely live up to

---

11. *Lutheran Study Bible*, 1620.

12. See chapters 3 and 4.

13. As one Bible commentary notes, "Genuine Christian humility will show itself in our attitude toward children. Jesus speaks of welcoming a little child in his name as a service done to him personally. We welcome a little child in Jesus' name, first of all, by recognizing that children are gifts of God, not grievous burdens. We serve Jesus by providing for the needs of children. That means not only food and shelter and clothing and loving care, but above all, bringing them to Jesus in Holy Baptism and training them to know and love

Jesus' words, good works performed by Christians in the service of children testifies to the "presence and indwelling" of the Holy Spirit (Formula of Concord: Epitome, Article IV, Good Works, in BC 499:15) and otherwise demonstrates that our faith is not dead (Jas 2:17).

Commenting on these verses, Martin Luther observes that this "picture should have hit them [the disciples] right in the eyes, to make them think 'Look! The great Lord of heaven and earth becomes like a little child. Why does he not embrace some great man, a king, or else a saint? Instead, he takes a child, and a tiny child at that, who still has very little understanding, and embraces him.'"[14]

Third, Jesus uses children as an illustration of divine wisdom. Jesus noted that God's path to salvation often escapes the "wise and intelligent" but God "reveals" divine truths even to infants (Matt 11:25). In making this claim, Jesus was asserting that our salvation is not dependent on our earthly wisdom but rather the faith effected in us by the Holy Spirit. When religious leaders scolded Jesus for receiving the praises of children, the Lord admonished the temple priests and scribes by noting "out of the mouths of infants and nursing babies you have prepared praise for yourself" (Matt 21:14–16). Jesus' assertion that God can give divine wisdom even to babies sharply contrasts with the Greco-Roman denigration of children for their lack of reason.[15]

Fourth, Jesus admonishes any in the church, including his closest disciples, for keeping children away from him (Mark 10:13–16). Commenting on these verses, Mark Paavola observes children "are not the marginal members of the Kingdom, but are the center."[16] Indeed, as noted at the outset, Jesus contends that children are God's messengers and that our treatment of boys and

---

and obey their Savior. . . . In many ways we can provide for the needs of little children in our church, in our community, and in other parts of the world." Albrecht and Albrecht, *Matthew*, 257.

14 Luther, *Annotations on Matthew*, 344.

15. See chapter 3, notes 1–3 and the accompanying text.

16. Paavola, *Mark*, 182.

girls speaks volumes about how we regard Jesus and, therefore, God (Mark 9:36–37).

Millstones and Angels: Jesus' Warning against Harming Children

In each of the Synoptic Gospels, Jesus issues a harsh warning against anyone who harms a child (Matt 18:6–9; Luke 17:1–2; Mark 9:42). Specifically, Jesus says, "If any of you put a stumbling block before one of these little ones who believe in me, it would be better for you if a great millstone were hung around your neck and you were thrown into the sea" (Mark 9:42). The phrase "little ones" comes from the Greek adjective *mikros* which, in this context, means the "smallest child."[17] The reference to "stumbling block" could be a reference to any sin but especially those sins that damage someone's faith.[18] The reference to "great millstone" is a reference to a stone turned in a mill by an animal, usually a donkey, to grind seed into flour.[19] Taken together, then, Jesus is saying that anything we do to hurt a child's faith is viewed by God in the harshest possible terms.[20]

According to some Bible scholars, Jesus may specifically be condemning the sin of sexual abuse.[21] William Loader, who has focused his work on sexuality in the New Testament world,[22] agrees with this analysis. Loader sees the phrase "little ones" in Mark 9:42

17. Paavola, *Mark*, 182.

18. Paavola, *Mark*, 182.

19. Paavola, *Mark*, 182.

20. This does not mean that abusing a child or failing to protect a child from abuse is an unforgiveable sin. It does, though, mean that we should take this sin seriously and seek God's help in turning away from it.

21. See Horsley's commentary on Mark in the *New Annotated Oxford Bible*, 1809n. This conclusion is based on this verse combined with subsequent verses pertaining to sins committed by various parts of the body and the Oxford Bible commentators' review of "references in rabbinic literature." (*New Annotated Oxford Bible*, 1809n).

22. E.g., Loader, *Making Sense of Sex*; Loader, *Sexuality and the Jesus Tradition*.

as "naturally" referring back to the child referenced six verses earlier (Mark 9:36).[23] This is because "there has been no indication of a change of scene in the narrative."[24]

To Loader, then, Mark "portrays Jesus as giving a stern warning about causing harm to children."[25] Loader calls the warning in 9:42 "extraordinary for its severity" but notes it parallels the warnings in 9:43–48 in which Jesus says it is better to cut off our hands or feet and gouge out our eyes rather than use these body parts to sin and endure hell. Since the hand, foot, and eye "can easily carry sexual connotations" and the foot "was an established euphemism for penis (Exod 4:25; Deut 28:56; Isa 6:2; 7:20),"[26] Loader believes Jesus is specifically referring to the sexual abuse of children.[27] Given that pederasty "was the focus of regular attention in both early Christianity and Judaism as they encountered the pagan world," Loader concludes:

> It makes sense then to read both 9:42 and 9:43–48 as addressing the issue of abuse of children, in particular, pederasty. It would have made sense to Mark's Jewish and Gentile readers, for whom it would have been one of the major scandals in the Gentile world and one which might easily find its way into the Christian community of Gentile converts.[28]

Adela Yarbro Collins[29] reaches a similar conclusion to Loader's. Yarbro Collins notes that the phrase "little ones" (Mark 9:42) is "first and foremost a synonym" for children or infants and thus the logical inference is that this phrase is referencing the children

---

23. Loader, *New Testament on Sexuality*, 121.

24. Loader, *Sexuality and the Jesus Tradition*, 22.

25. Loader, *New Testament on Sexuality*, 121.

26. In other writings, Loader also cites Ruth 3:4, 7, 8, 14. Loader, *Sexuality and the Jesus Tradition*, 22.

27. Loader, *New Testament on Sexuality*, 123.

28. Loader, *New Testament on Sexuality*, 123.

29. Yarbro Collins is the Buckingham Professor of New Testament Criticism and Interpretation at the Yale University Divinity School.

discussed in vv. 36–37.[30] Yarbro Collins sees the phrase "who trust in me" (v. 42)[31] as an additional indicator that children are the focus of the text[32] and contends the phrase "giving offense," at least in this context, "probably means relating to a child in a sexual manner."[33]

If this is true, Yarbro Collins asserts the subsequent verses (43–48) "have sexuality as their primary referent."[34] With respect to the harsh language of "better a millstone" (Mark 9:42), Yarbro Collins interprets the verse to mean "it would be better for a person who molests a child to die the horrible death described than to face the final judgment without having been punished for the sin already."[35] According to Yarbro Collins, "The logic seems to be that punishment in this life is better than eternal punishment."[36]

If Yarbro Collins's interpretation is correct, then Jesus' words are remarkably consistent with what modern researchers and sex offender treatment providers tell us about serial sex offenders who prey on children. Sex offenders fitting into this category are extraordinarily manipulative, have significant cognitive distortions, and often need meaningful consequences such as prison in order to grasp the reality of their crimes.[37] In theological terms, offenders of this type need a strong application of the law before they are ready to receive the gospel.[38]

Not every commentator adopts the view held by Loader or Yarbro Collins, at least not in its entirety. For instance, Joel Marcus believes the reference to welcoming a child in Jesus' name (Mark 9:36) may partly reflect the reality of child exposure at the time

30. Yarbro Collins, *Mark*, 450.

31. The NRSV, NIV, and ESV translation of this verse is "who believe in me."

32. Yarbro Collins, *Mark*, 450.

33. Yarbro Collins, *Mark*, 450.

34. Yarbro Collins, *Mark*, 450.

35. Yarbro Collins, *Mark*, 450.

36. Yarbro Collins, *Mark*, 450.

37. Vieth, *What Would Walther Do?*, 261–64.

38. Vieth, *What Would Walther Do?*, 270–72.

and notes this would be consistent with "many early Christian texts" exhorting kindness to abandoned or orphaned children.[39] Nonetheless, Marcus believes the phrase "little ones" (Mark 9: 42) is "probably a term for the Christian community" and disagrees with the assertion the references to hand, foot, or eye (Mark 9:43–47) necessarily have a sexual meaning.[40] Marcus contends, for example, the "more usual and direct connotation" of foot is simply as a metaphor for walking, albeit possibly to a place where sins are committed.[41]

Even if the conclusion is that Jesus is not specifically referencing sexual abuse in this text, there is overwhelming evidence that child abuse impairs the faith of a child[42] and that Jesus' words can be read as an unequivocal condemnation of child maltreatment. John Schuetze[43] writes:

> Child abuse causes children to stumble in the faith in many ways. Later in life it can trigger sinful behavior to cope with the painful memories. It often confuses the person spiritually and theologically: "If there is a God, why didn't [God] help me? If God promises to answer our prayers, then why didn't [God] stop my abuse? I prayed about it many times."[44]

From this, Schuetze concludes, "Jesus recognized children were valuable and vulnerable" and that for this very reason Christ issued the "strong warning" contained in the Synoptic Gospels.[45]

There is a second, equally harsh reference Jesus makes to hurting children, especially a child's faith. As recorded in the Gospel of Matthew, we must "take care" so that we "do not despise one of these little ones; for, I tell you, in heaven their angels continuously see the face of my Father in heaven" (Matt 18:10). Although many

39. Marcus, *Mark 8–16*, 682.

40. Marcus, *Mark 8–16*, 689–91.

41. Marcus, *Mark 8–16*, 691.

42. Walker et al., "Addressing Religious and Spiritual Issues," 174.

43. John Schuetze is a seminary professor at Wisconsin Lutheran Seminary.

44. Schuetze, "Pastoral Theology Brief," 224.

45. Schuetze, "Pastoral Theology Brief," 224.

biblical scholars contend that "little ones" refers to any believer,[46] other scholars connect the phrase primarily to children.[47] C. F. W. Walther[48] belonged in this narrower camp, contending the "text teaches us that God has commended to the angels the guardianship of our dear, weak, and often needy children."[49]

Although acknowledging the broader interpretation as plausible, Martin Luther concluded the better interpretation is that Christ is specifically referring to children.[50] According to Luther, "God lays these very youth in our laps" and commends them to our care.[51] Contending God has "such zeal for the little children," Luther says the Lord "does not have them each guarded with a gun or pike, but gives them great lords and princes as guardians to protect them, namely, the dear angels, who watch over the child against the devil, the evil angel."[52] Accordingly, if we are "not in awe of the children, then be in awe of their protectors."[53]

Working to a crescendo, Luther writes:

> We Christians . . . ought not to esteem the children as being so poor and lowly, but rather we ought to open our spiritual eyes and consider how the little children are surrounded by such tremendously great princes and lords. . . . This should constantly move us to refrain from doing or saying anything in their presence that would lead them astray. And if you were able with your physical

46. E.g., *NIV Study Bible* (Zondervan, 2011), 1622 (noting that guardian angels are "not exclusively for children, but for God's people in general"); *Lutheran Study Bible* (Concordia, 2009), 1621 (contending the reference is to any "fellow believer").

47. Albrecht and Albrecht, *Matthew*, 259.

48. C. F. W. Walther was the first president of the Lutheran Church Missouri Synod and he guided the young church through a major sexual abuse scandal involving a bishop who sexually exploited a number of young women. Walther's most influential theological writing was a treatise on the application of law and gospel. See generally, Suelflow, *Servant of the Word*.

49. Walther, *God Grant It*, 908.

50. Luther, *Annotations on Matthew*, 375.

51. Luther, *Annotations on Matthew*, 375.

52. Luther, *Annotations on Matthew*, 376.

53. Luther, *Annotations on Matthew*, 376.

eyes to see one child's guardian, a single angel, then you would be in greater awe before that child than before a king.[54]

"I Never Knew You"—Christ's Promised Judgment against Those Failing to Care for the Suffering

When speaking of the Day of Judgment, Christ promises to welcome those who gave food, drink, and clothing to the "least of these" who Christ calls "members of my family" (Matt 25:34–40). In a similar vein, Christ promises to cast aside those who failed to care for those who are suffering because "just as you did not do it to one of the least of these, you did not do it to me" (Matt 25:45). Since many maltreated children are denied food, water, clothing, medical care, and other necessities of life, conduct that often meets the medical definition of torture,[55] it is easy to also apply these strong words to instances of abuse.

54. Luther, *Annotations on Matthew*, 377.
55. Knox et al., "Child Torture," 37–49.

7

Child Abuse and Christ
What Did Jesus Know
and When Did He Know It?

WHY WAS JESUS SO strong in his statements about children? Why
is it that our treatment of children—as opposed to adults, elders,
or those suffering from poverty, disease, or injustice—should be
the benchmark for evaluating our love of God (Mark 9:36–37)?[1]
As noted by Loader and other scholars, concerns of pederasty and
infanticide at the time of Christ may certainly have been one reason Jesus raised his voice. There is, though, a more compelling and
transforming reason—Jesus is the very Son of God who, according
to Scripture and the Lutheran Confessions possesses "incompre-
hensible wisdom" (Formula of Concord, Article VII, BCV 601:47).
As humanity grows its knowledge through ACE and spiritual
injury research, as well as sex offender studies, we gain a deeper
insight into the depth of Jesus' wisdom in his concern for children

---

1. "Throughout the Synoptics, there are many who come to Jesus, including those who are unclean, poor, beggars, Gentiles, women, and sinners.
However, at no point does Jesus choose one of these as a sign of the kingdom
of heaven by placing them in the midst of the disciples." White, "He Placed a
Little Child in the Midst," 353.

and also his engagement with the sinful condition of humankind, a condition which only God fully understands.

According to the "Formula of Concord," in the Lutheran Confessions, it is an "essential characteristic" of Christ's divine nature for Jesus to "know all things" (Formula of Concord, Article VIII, BC 617:9).[2] Although Jesus was also true man, the Lutheran Confessions assert "nothing was added or taken away from his divine nature in its essence or characteristics through the incarnation. It became neither smaller nor greater in and of itself through the incarnation" (Formula of Concord, Article VIII, BC 624:48). "The result," the Formula of Concord asserts, "is not that he knows some things while not knowing other things, or that he can do some things while not being able to do others, but that he knows and can do all things" (Formula of Concord, Article X, BC 639:73).

In addition to Christ's divine knowledge of the prevalence and temporal and eternal consequences of child abuse, Jesus' humanity inexorably connects him to the suffering of children.[3] In discussing the humanity of Christ, the Formula of Concord contends that Jesus "also promised that he would be present—he, the human being who had spoken with them, who had experienced every tribulation in the assumed human nature, who for this reason can have sympathy with us as fellow human beings" (Formula of Concord, Article VIII, BC 633:87).

God's understanding of the suffering of children is decisively and definitively manifest in the suffering and death of Jesus. In

2. Throughout this paper, "BC" refers to the "Book of Concord." This will be followed by a reference to the page and paragraph number. Accordingly, the citation 617:9 refers to page 617, paragraph 9. Robert Kolb and Timothy J. Wengert, eds. *The Book of Concord: The Confessions of the Evangelical Lutheran Church* (Minneapolis: Fortress Press 2000).

3. Lutheran teaching on the two natures of Christ is grounded in the concept of "communicatio idiomatum" which asserts the "union between the divine and human natures in the person of Christ is a much different, higher, indescribable communion. Because of this union and communion God is a human being and a human being is God. Nevertheless, through this union and communion neither the natures nor their characteristics are mixed together with the other, but each nature retains its own essence and characteristics." Formula of Concord, Article VIII, BC 619:19.

Confessing the One Faith (*COF*), the ecumenical scholars, who had gathered under the auspices of the World Council of Churches to study and compose an explication of the Nicene-Constantinopolitan Creed, declare a critical consensus about the crucifixion of Jesus. Specifically, the *COF* asserts Jesus not only paid for our sins but that through the cross "God is demonstrating to human beings that he is with them in these situations, that he is suffering where they are suffering—especially where there is no apparent reason in such suffering—and thereby gives them consolation and strength."[4]

Confessing the One Faith makes two additional points about the passion history that is relevant to instances of child maltreatment. First, the text asserts the crucifixion ensures victims of "God's solidarity" with them.[5] "In the particular case of oppression," the *COF* maintains, "the victim is assured that God is never on the side of the oppressor, the bringer of death, but will, in his justice, protect the rights and lives of the victims."[6] Second, the fact that Jesus overcame both suffering and death gives hope to all who suffer. It is asserted in *Confessing the One Faith* that the "apparent weakness of God proved to be stronger than the powers of this world."[7]

In the context of child abuse, there is ample reason to believe Christ "can have sympathy" (BC 633:87) with many survivors. Christ was physically struck (John 18:22), emotionally abused (John 19:2–3; Luke 23:35–36), disowned by his closest friends (Luke 22:60–61), the recipient of corporal punishment (John 19:1), and tortured to death (Luke 23:26–46). In addition to having endured multiple forms of abuse, Christ "wants to be with us in all our troubles" because by his very nature Jesus "is our brother and we are flesh of his flesh" (Formula of Concord, Article VIII, BC 633:87).

---

4. WCC, *Confessing the One Faith*, 50.
5. WCC, *Confessing the One Faith*, 50.
6. WCC, *Confessing the One Faith*, 50.
7. WCC, *Confessing the One Faith*, 51.

In other words, every child who has ever lived or will live is the brother or sister of Christ, the very "flesh of his flesh" (Formula of Concord, Article VIII, BC 633:87). This means that every blow administered to their bodies, every sexual violation, every act of starvation, every refusal of medical care, is both a blatant affront to God who sent them (Mark 9:36–37) and the purposeful infliction of suffering on Christ (Matt 25:45). Indeed, those who stand on the sidelines, who fail to raise their voices or extend their hands to suffering children are rejecting the Son of Man, Jesus the Christ (Matt 25:45–46).[8]

It is that simple—and that profound.

---

8. There is, of course, hope for both child abusers and those who enable child abusers. Although God's law is a "thunderbolt" that "destroys both the open sinner and the false saint" (BC 312:2), it is not the end of the story. The purpose of the law is to convict us of our sins so that we may turn to Christ for forgiveness (BC 313:4–9).

8

Early Christian Responses
to Child Abuse

THERE IS EVIDENCE THAT the early church took seriously Jesus' condemnation of child abuse and responded in both doctrine and conduct.[1] In terms of doctrine, the early Christians "consistently upheld the condemnation of sexual relations between children and adults."[2] In 180 CE, Bishop Theophilus of Antioch wrote that those who "corrupt boys" or sell their children do not know God.[3] Early "ecclesiastical councils and theologians considered pederasty a sin that entailed exclusion from the Christian community."[4] Simply stated, the "Christian sexual ethic" was a "clear break with the view of sexual relations between adults and children in the Greco-Roman tradition."[5]

1. At all times, including the present, the church has acknowledged most forms of child abuse to be sinful. What distinguishes the early church, though, is the fact the opposition to abuse was vehement, countercultural, and impacted both church and society. See chapter 8, notes 1–13 and accompanying text.

2. Bakke, *When Children Became People*, 140.

3. Bakke, *When Children Became People*, 140.

4. Bakke, *When Children Became People*, 141.

5. Bakke, *When Children Became People*, 144.

In terms of actual conduct, O. M. Bakke concludes the early church brought about a "dramatic decline" in the number of children, particularly boys, who were sexually abused.[6] Citing early Christian household codes (e.g., Col 3:20–4:1), particularly as they may apply to slave children, Margaret MacDonald concludes the "theological implications" of these codes "implies an ethical imperative that warns against believing masters making sexual use of slaves in the community."[7]

This influence extended beyond sexual abuse. According to Paul Offit, early church leaders contended that children were important to God and "shouldn't be killed, maimed or abused."[8] Despite the many references to children, the only New Testament reference to the discipline of children (Eph 6:4; Col 3:21) encourages parents not to exasperate their children—a message that was countercultural to the harsh corporal punishment of the era.[9] The early church pressured the state to protect children which led to the criminalizing of infanticide by Constantine and then, in 321 CE, providing relief to poor parents so they wouldn't have to sell their children.[10]

Gregory Henry Payne writes:

> Amid all the differences of opinion and doctrine that we find among the early founders of Christianity, there was one thing on which they were unanimous, and that was the attitude toward children. It was a ceaseless war they waged on behalf of children—those early and oftentimes eloquent founders. From Barnabas, contemporary of the Apostles, to Ambrosius and Augustine, they did not cease to denounce those who, no matter what their reasons, exposed or killed children.[11]

6. Bakke, *When Children Became People*, 151.

7. MacDonald, *Power of Children*, 152.

8. Offit, *Bad Faith*, 126.

9. Joersz, *Galatians, Ephesians & Philippians*, 161.

10. Offit, *Bad Faith*, 127.

11. Payne, *Child in Human Progress*, 258.

Not every scholar believes the early Christians were universally or uniquely committed to ending child abuse. For example, Christian Laes notes that early Christian opposition to pederasty was shared by some "pagan contemporaries" and may have been rooted more out of opposition to homosexuality than concern for children.[12] Nonetheless, Laes concedes the early Christians were "radically opposed" to pederasty and quotes Karl Marx as concluding "we can forgive Christians much, for they taught us how to love children."[13]

In the centuries that followed, as the distance between the church and Christ's time on earth grew, Christians ceased to be a dominant force in the fight against child abuse. Even worse, the church often found itself as a contributor to the physical abuse, sexual abuse, and neglect of children.[14]

12. Laes, *Children in the Roman Empire*, 268.
13. Laes, *Children in the Roman Empire*, 269.
14. See chapter 9, notes 1–35 and accompanying text.

9

Modern Christian Responses
to Child Abuse

To GET A SENSE of how far the Christian community has strayed
from Christ's call to protect children, a number of sexual abuse
scandals and false doctrines paint a picture of a church in need
of reform. Christian scandals, false doctrines, and blatant indif-
ference have contributed to the abuse of countless children and
stained the name of Jesus.

CHILD SEXUAL ABUSE SCANDALS: CATHOLIC
COMMUNITIES

The United States Conference of Catholic Bishops selected John Jay
College to assess the scope of sexual abuse of children by Catholic
Priests and Deacons in the United States during the years 1950–
2002. The report concluded the "prevalence of the problem in the
Catholic Church" was "widespread" with more than 95 percent of
the US dioceses impacted.[1] Every region of the United States aver-
aged between 3 percent and 6 percent of their priests accused of

---

1. John Jay College, "Nature and Scope of Sexual Abuse," 26.

sexual abuse.[2] By 2012, American Catholic Bishops counted more than 6,100 priests as credibly accused of sexually abusing children since 1950—which accounted for 5.6 percent of the total priests serving during that time period.[3] There are several reasons to believe these numbers are *low*. First, the information provided was based in part on personnel files which may have been incomplete or had records removed.[4] Second, the study was only of known allegations and, since many victims never disclose abuse, the "number of allegations is lower than the number of actual incidents."[5]

Similar sexual abuse scandals occurred in the Catholic community throughout the world.[6] Although this has spurred a number of reforms in the church,[7] the reforms have been largely driven by lawsuits and the media[8] as opposed to the theological reform[9] contemplated in this paper.[10]

2. John Jay College, "Nature and Scope of Sexual Abuse," 27.

3. D'Antonio, *Mortal Sins*, 301.

4. Lytton, *Holding Bishops Accountable*, 44.

5. Lytton, *Holding Bishops Accountable*, 43.

6. D'Antonio, *Mortal Sins*, 202–3, 262, 291, 323–24, 327, 331–32.

7. Terry et al., *Causes and Context*, 120.

8. See generally, Lytton, *Holding Bishops Accountable*.

9. Calling it an "irony," Mary Ann Hinsdale observes that "despite its many statements on the family, Roman Catholic teaching has given little systematic consideration to the child." Hinsdale, "Infinite Openness," 406.

10. In interpreting Mark 9:36–37, in which Jesus calls children his messengers and contends the treatment of children reflects our view of God, the Catholic Study Bible contends the words of Jesus pertain not so much to children but to Christ's disciples. Specifically, the commentary states: "Mark probably intends this incident and the sayings that follow as commentary on the disciples' lack of understanding (Mark 9:32). Their role in Jesus' work is one of service, especially to the poor and lowly. Children were the symbol Jesus used for the *anawin*, the poor in spirit, the lowly in the Christian community." *Catholic Teen Bible*, 86 NT. If Jesus was not using children merely as a symbol, but was actually and vociferously condemning the abuse of children (as some commentators contend), would this different interpretation have lessened the sexual abuse scandal detailed in the John Jay study? Would a different reading of the text change the future direction of the church?

CHILD SEXUAL ABUSE SCANDALS: PROTESTANT COMMUNITIES

Although there is "no comparable information base" to study the extent of sexual abuse in other Christian denominations,[11] the Protestant community is not immune to child sexual abuse scandals. In recent decades, Protestants have seen scandals in New Tribes Mission,[12] the Christian Missionary Alliance,[13] ABWE,[14] and Bob Jones University.[15] There have also been hundreds of media accounts of Protestant church leaders arrested or convicted of sexually abusing children.[16] According to three insurance companies that insure a majority of Protestant congregations in the United States, there are approximately 260 annual reports of children being sexually abused by ministers or other church workers.[17] In 2012, Christian radio host Janet Mefferd contended, "This is an epidemic going on in churches. . . . When are evangelicals going to wake up and say we have a massive problem in our own churches?"[18]

CHRISTIAN TEACHINGS THAT HAVE CONTRIBUTED TO CHILD ABUSE AND NEGLECT

In addition to sexual abuse scandals, there are a number of "Christian" teachings, some arising within sects and some within mainstream Christendom, that have contributed to the neglect and abuse of children. Even when a teaching that contributes to child maltreatment is extreme or not adhered to by the majority of Christians, the failure of the mainstream church to speak against

11. Lytton, *Holding Bishops Accountable*, 10.

12. GRACE, *Final Report*.

13. See *All God's Children* (documentary).

14. Zylstra, "Missionary Donn Ketcham."

15. Pérez-Peña, "Bob Jones University Blamed Victims."

16. GRACE, "Startling News."

17. Associated Press, "Data Shed Light on Child Sexual Abuse."

18. Joyce, "By Grace Alone."

these teachings stands as a polar opposite to the strong voice of Jesus (e.g., Matt 18:6).

Medical Neglect of Children

In any given year, "tens of thousands of Americans refuse medical care for their children in the name of God."[19] Consider, for example, the fate of Brandon Schaible, a seven-month-old baby who died from pneumonia because his parents belonged to a Christian church which interpreted James 5:14–15 as requiring sick children to be taken for prayer by elders and not to a hospital for treatment.[20] This was the second child allowed to die as a result of the parents' reliance exclusively on prayer as opposed to the medical care God has provided us.[21]

Physical Abuse of Children

In the United States, more than 50 percent of substantiated physical abuse cases start out as an attempt at physical discipline and they end up in bruises, blood, broken bones, and sometimes death.[22] Although five decades of research has found that corporal punishment is the least effective form of discipline and is associated with significant risk factors,[23] many prominent Christians have distorted a handful of proverbs to insist the Bible *requires* parents to discipline their children by hitting them.[24] Christian books advocating for the corporal punishment of children have

19. Offit, *Bad Faith*, ix.

20. Offit, *Bad Faith*, ix.

21. Offit, *Bad Faith*, ix.

22. Gershoff, *Report on Physical Punishment in the United States*.

23. Gershoff and Grogran-Kaylor, "Spanking and Child Outcomes," 453.

24. For example, Albert Mohler, president of the Southern Baptist Theological Seminary, writes, "Does the Bible instruct parents to spank their children? The answer to that must be an emphatic, Yes. Though the words 'spare the rod and spoil the child' do not appear in the biblical text, the Bible makes the same point in an unmistakable way." Mohler, *Should Spanking Be Banned?*

sold millions of copies[25] and some of these books admonish parents to begin striking children as infants.[26]

As a result of these teachings, hitting children as a means of discipline is much more widely accepted in conservative Christian circles than in other communities.[27] In an editorial published in 2014, the board of editors of *Christianity Today* noted the contribution of Christian teachings to the physical abuse and death of a number of children and urged the church to reevaluate its teachings in the light of Scripture,[28] parenting research,[29] and common sense.[30] When the theological underpinnings of corporal punishment are challenged with alternative views of these Bible passages, researchers from Pepperdine University have found that many conservative Protestants change their attitudes about physical discipline.[31]

Sexual Abuse of Children

Two Bible verses have often been cited in a way that harms sexually abused children or contributes to their victimization. First, the admonition in the book of Romans to "counsel one another" (Rom 15:4), has been used by some Christian churches to discourage survivors of child abuse from obtaining competent mental

---

25. E.g., Dobson, *New Dare to Discipline*.

26. E.g., Pearl and Pearl, *To Train Up a Child*.

27. Hoffman et al., "Conservative Protestantism"; Enten, "Americans' Opinions on Spanking."

28. For a thorough analysis and biblically sound rejection of the belief the Bible requires parents to discipline their children by hitting them, see Webb, *Corporal Punishment in the Bible*; Vieth, "Providing Pastoral Guidance," 31.

29. American Academy of Pediatrics, "Guidance for Effective Discipline," 723.

30. *Christianity Today*, "Thou Shall Not Abuse."

31. Miller-Perrin and Perrin, "Changing Attitudes about Spanking"; Perrin et al., "Changing Attitudes about Spanking," 514.

health services[32] that often prove critical in their recovery from maltreatment.[33]

Second, the admonition in Matthew 18:15–18 to speak privately with an erring Christian has been used by Christian pastors and laity to avoid reporting a case of child sexual abuse to the authorities.[34] This may happen when a pastor hears an outcry of child abuse but, based on his or her reading of these passages in Matthew, decides to first speak with the alleged offender. If the offender denies the abuse or "repents" some pastors conclude the matter is resolved (Matt 18:15). In other instances, pastors have used these passages to urge a victim to first confront his or her abuser (Matt 18:15)—a suggestion that shifts the burden of protection from the church to the child victim.[35]

THE CHOICES WE'VE MADE

Inadequate Training

Although lawsuits and bad press have raised awareness among Christians as to the prevalence of child abuse, very few Christian seminaries or denominations require any training on the subject.[36] In a 2015 study of the course catalogues of every accredited

32. Instead, some Christian churches encourage survivors of abuse to pursue a biblical form of counseling known as "Nouthetic" counseling. For additional information, see the Institute for Nouthetic Studies, http://www.nouthetic.org.

33. Noting that approximately two-thirds of victims of child sexual abuse will experience post-traumatic stress disorder symptoms at some point in their life, Terri Watson concludes that "most" survivors will need a referral to a qualified mental health professional. Watson, "Counseling the Abuse Victim," 248–49, 259.

34. Schuetze, "Pastoral Theology Brief," 224.

35. Sex offenders have significant cognitive distortions that even seasoned treatment providers struggle to address. Requiring a victim, particularly a child victim, to confront such a person is not simply unrealistic, it is cruel. For an analysis of cognitive distortions by clergy abusers of children, see Terry et al., *Causes and Context of Sexual Abuse*, 103–13.

36. Vieth, "Keeping the Faith," 947.

seminary in the United States, researchers found only 3 percent of seminaries had a focused course on child maltreatment.[37]

Inadequate Policies

Lawsuits and media attention have forced a number of churches to implement child protection policies.[38] Unfortunately, these policies often focus only on preventing sexual abuse within the church since that is the only form of abuse that has resulted in litigation.[39] In other words, sexual abuse in the home, as well as physical abuse, emotional abuse, neglect, or witnessing violence is seldom the focus of policies or training even though many church leaders are mandated reporters.[40]

Failing to Reach the Suffering

Over the years, hundreds of adult survivors of abuse have shared with me their struggle to return to church.[41] Some were beaten and are afraid to return to any church that clings to the notion that children must be hit. Others were sexually violated but can't find a church whose faith in Christ is acted out (Jas 2:17) through rigorous child protection policies and training. One man told me he used to listen every week to the podcasts of area preachers hoping he would hear a sermon about child abuse and know which church would welcome him. He never heard such a sermon and, after several years of trying, he just gave up.

Although it's a minority view, some scholars note the plausibility of reading all of Matthew 18:1–14 as references to child maltreatment.[42] If this is so, then Jesus' plea to find the lost sheep

37. Betz, "Analysis of Child Abuse Training."

38. Lytton, *Holding Bishops Accountable*.

39. Vieth, "Suffer the Children," 1.

40. Child Welfare Information Gateway, "Clergy as Mandated Reporters."

41. Vieth, "When Is It Safe."

42. Loader, *New Testament on Sexuality*, 125–27.

who have "gone astray" (Matt 18:12–14), is a plea to pursue abused children who have been pushed away from church and from God.[43] Whether or not these passages apply only to abused children, certainly the language is broad enough to be read as an admonition to develop ministries of care for abused and neglected children. Although some Christian denominations have done exactly that,[44] it is not yet the norm in all Christian communities.

43. Describing the impact of being sexually abused by a priest and being shunned by the church, one survivor writes "I felt it was God's representative on earth that opened my eyes to God's failing. I don't believe in God today at all. . . . I grew to hate the smells, sounds, feelings of the Church—the incense, the collars, the robes. My spirituality and ability to believe in a higher power were destroyed." Frawley-Odea, "God Images in Clinical Work."

44. The Wisconsin Evangelical Lutheran Synod (WELS), for example, has started a ministry for families impacted by abuse entitled Freedom for the Captives. The ministry can be accessed at www.freedomforcaptives.com.

10

Centering Christian Responses to Child Abuse on the Words of Christ

IN COMMENTING ON CHRIST'S words that whoever welcomes a child welcomes Jesus and God (Mark 9:37), Wess Stafford[1] suspects the disciples were "stunned and reeling as Jesus' words sank in—an act of kindness to a child is the same thing as doing that act to Jesus Christ—indeed, to God himself?"[2] Stafford then paints a picture of how the church should have responded—and how he believes the church actually responded:

> One would think that a great new respect and appreciation for children would have seized their hearts. A whole new theology should have arisen that placed children at the center of the work of the church. A new priority

---

1. Dr. Wess Stafford is the president and CEO of Compassion International. He is also a survivor of child physical and sexual abuse at the hands of Christian missionaries. Recalling these experiences, Stafford writes, "Why did God let me suffer the agonies of that boarding school? Why did he not intervene when I cried out to him night after night for relief? I have imagined at times my guardian angel pulling on God's sleeve saying, 'Don't you hear little Wesley? Don't you see his pitiful tears? Can't you do something to deliver him from this monstrous evil?'" Stafford, *Too Small to Ignore*, 158.

2. Stafford, *Too Small to Ignore*, 204.

for programs, budgets, and strategies should have been established that very moment.

> How unbelievable that they [the disciples] forgot all this within a few days. How unbelievably sad that the church would also forget this for the next two thousand years.[3]

Although Stafford's words are powerful and reflect the experiences of many survivors of abuse, he may be overstating the case. As noted earlier, there is evidence early Christians may have taken seriously Christ's words as applied to instances of child abuse and acted to protect these children. If this is true, perhaps the church doesn't need to do anything new but simply needs to turn again to the Bible and see what the Scriptures generally, and Christ in particular, have to say about children and the sin of child abuse.

CHILD MALTREATMENT AND SCRIPTURE

Applying the Ten Commandments to a Representative Case of Child Abuse

Although some scholars have compiled a lengthy list of Bible verses directly or indirectly condemning one or more forms of child maltreatment,[4] there is not a single act of child abuse that escapes the prohibition of the Ten Commandments. Indeed, a typical case of child maltreatment violates *each* of the commandments given by God to Moses (Exod 20). Consider, for example, this hypothetical but typical case of child maltreatment:[5]

> My dad used to beat me with a stick engraved with Bible verses. He also touched me sexually and then said I was equally sinful because I had an erection. His favorite time to abuse me was Sunday morning so that we could go to

3. Stafford, *Too Small to Ignore*, 204.

4. Tracy, *Mending the Soul*, 217–23.

5. Two-thirds of abused children are maltreated in at least two ways and approximately one-third are abused in five or more ways. Turner et al., "Poly-victimization," 323; Finkelhor et al., "Poly-victimization," *Journal of Child*, 7.

church together and be "forgiven." He told me I couldn't tell Mom because she was weak and would only make things worse. He often "borrowed" my allowance to buy porn to show me what to do to him. My Dad used to tell me he craved my pure heart but, since he couldn't have one of his own, he said he had to make sure he crushed mine. When he was charged with a crime years later, he testified under oath that I was a liar. I wasn't a liar, my Dad was.

In one paragraph, this abuse scenario contravenes the entire law of God. The offender violated the First Commandment by placing sexual abuse above God (Exod 20:3)—an act of idolatry.[6] He violated the Second Commandment by using the Bible in the abuse of a child (Exod 20:7). The Third Commandment was violated when the child was abused on the Sabbath (Exod 20:8). The Fourth Commandment to honor parents was abridged when the child was encouraged not to turn to his mother for help (Exod 20:12). The Fifth Commandment fell when the child was beaten (Exod 20:13). Every act of sexual abuse ran counter to the Sixth Commandment (Exod 20:14). The Seventh Commandment was violated when the child's allowance was "borrowed" (Exod 20:15). The Eighth Commandment prohibition against bearing false witness was violated when the offender lied about his son in court (Exod 20:16). The Ninth and Tenth commandments against coveting were obliterated when the offender craved his son's pure heart and, when he couldn't have such a heart, destroyed his son's (Exod 20:17).

In explaining these commandments, Martin Luther believed that for every "shalt not" there was a corresponding "shalt"

---

6. According to Martin Luther, "Idolatry does not consist merely of erecting an image and praying to it, but it is primarily a matter of the heart, which fixes its gaze upon other things and seeks help and consolation from creatures, saints or devils. It neither cares for God nor expects good things from him sufficiently to trust that he wants to help, nor does it believe that whatever good it encounters comes from God." Luther, "Large Catechism," in Kolb and Wengert, Book of Concord, 388.

Christians must take to heart.[7] In the context of child abuse, then, it is not enough to refrain from beating, raping, or starving children, the obligations of parents and the church is to proactively protect children from abuse.[8]

Applying the Words of Jesus to a Typical Case of Child Abuse

When asked which is the greatest commandment, Jesus encapsulated the law into two obligations—to love God with all our heart, soul, and mind, and love our neighbor as we love ourselves (Matt 22:36–40).[9] On these commandments, Jesus said, "hang all the law and the prophets" (Matt 23:40). Mark's Gospel has a slightly different wording in which Jesus contends these are the "first" and "second" commandments and asserts "there is no commandment greater than these" (Mark 12:28–31).

If it is true that children are God's messengers[10] and that our treatment of them determines how much we value God (Mark 9:36–37), then any act of child abuse is a violation of the "greatest commandment." Similarly, since we would never beat, rape, starve, or humiliate ourselves, then any act of child abuse violates the second greatest commandment.

---

7. Wengert, *Martin Luther's Catechisms*, 31.

8. Wengert, *Martin Luther's Catechisms*, 35.

9. In the Gospel of Mark, a scribe asks Jesus which commandment is "first of all" and Jesus responds by labeling love of God and love of neighbor as the "first" and "second" commandments (Mark 12:28–31).

10. Obviously, God can and does use adults as messengers as well. The illustration in the Gospel of Mark allowed Jesus to "emphasize service and humility" and to note that even those who appear insignificant are treasured by God. Paavola, *Mark*, 170. In this paper, though, the argument is that Jesus may also have used children as an object lesson fully recognizing the harsh discipline, exposure, infanticide, slavery, and sexual abuse faced by children in the Greco-Roman era as well as contemporary society.

JESUS AND CHILDREN: THE "NEW" OLD CHURCH

If Christians everywhere returned in earnest to the Gospel accounts of Jesus and the children and applied these words to the contemporary church, what would be different? Perhaps the possibilities are best explored through the following hypothetical:

> In giving his report on insurance rates to his fellow church elders, John details his discussion with various insurance carriers. "It appears," John says, "we could lower our church liability insurance by 10% if we had background checks on our pastors, Sunday School teachers, coaches and volunteers who work with youth. The cost of a background check is about $15 a person and this would need to be done on about 100 people."
>
> After discussing the issue for an hour, the church elders decide not to incur this additional expense and cite five reasons. First, managing that many background checks would require additional administrative support that is not practical for the church at this time. Second, the savings to the church from the lower insurance rate would be offset by the additional expense of paying for so many background checks. Third, most of those working with children have done so for years and all the elders are confident none of them could be a child abuser. Fourth, many people would be offended by having to do a background check and some might be so upset the church would lose badly needed volunteers. Fifth, there was concern that someone might have a DWI or other conviction that would be embarrassing if discovered and the elders felt it was sinful to force people to reveal such private matters.

How might this conversation have been different if the elders focused on the words of Jesus in Mark 9:36–37 and 42? Perhaps the elders would have concluded that children are extremely important to Jesus and that a faithful response to Christ's words would include at least minimal actions to keep them safe within the church. Perhaps concern about protecting children from abuse would have been elevated above concerns for administrative burdens, or the embarrassment or harsh reactions from volunteers. Perhaps the cost to a child of being abused would have outweighed the cost of paying for background checks.

Although there is no telling what the Holy Spirit unleashed might do for children, placing Jesus' words about children at the forefront of our minds might lead to at least ten reforms. Implementing even one of these reforms would improve the lot of children. Implementing all ten would radically transform the church.[11]

First, every seminary should implement a rigorous course on child maltreatment. This class would include education on recognizing and responding to all forms of child abuse and coordinating pastoral care with child protection agencies as well as medical and mental health professionals.[12] In addition to seminaries, Christian universities and colleges should implement the recommendation of the United States Department of Justice, contained in a national study on family violence, to dramatically improve the undergraduate training of professionals working with maltreated children.[13]

Second, every church should have child protection policies that meet national standards promulgated by the Centers for Disease Control for youth-serving organizations.[14] Indeed, a true Christian witness would shatter these minimal standards and also implement policies to address not only sexual abuse within the church[15] but also sexual abuse in the home, as well as physical abuse, neglect, emotional abuse, and witnessing violence.[16] The organization GRACE (Godly Response to the Christian Environment) has published a comprehensive book that walks congregational leaders through the development and implementa-

11. This list is, in part, adapted from Vieth, "Ten Things the Church Can Do."

12. The organization GRACE (Godly Response to Abuse in the Christian Environment) and the Gundersen National Child Protection Training Center have in fact developed such a course and, at this writing, are looking for seminary partners to implement the program.

13. US Dept. of Justice, *Executive Summary*, 6.

14. Saul and Audage, *Preventing Child Sexual Abuse*.

15. Reju, *On Guard*.

16. Vieth, "Suffer the Children," 1.

tion of child protection policies addressing all forms of abuse in the home, church, or elsewhere.[17] This is one of many resources God has given the modern church to assist in keeping children safe—and there is no excuse for failing to act.

Third, as part of its policies, every church should require child abuse training for all staff and volunteers who work with children as well as personal safety training for all children attending church schools, camps, sports, or other activities.[18]

Fourth, every church would have policies to assist in monitoring convicted sex offenders attending services or other church activities.[19] Beyond these policies, pastoral-care workers should receive education on ministering to sex offenders and coordinating this work with sex offender treatment providers.[20]

Fifth, every pastor should periodically preach a sermon on one or more aspects of child maltreatment as well as offer Bible studies on the subject. This is the message from God's word that countless children are waiting to hear[21]—and the church has long delayed in preaching.[22]

Sixth, the church must break its silence against false doctrines that have contributed to the physical abuse of children,[23] the withholding of medical care, and that has kept survivors from accessing quality mental health care. Although speaking out may offend

17. Tchividjian and Berkovits, *Child Safeguarding Policy Guide.*

18 Wurtele and Kenny, "Primary Prevention of Child Sexual Abuse," 107; Finkelhor, "Prevention of Sexual Abuse," 640.

19. Vieth, "Suffer the Children," 1.

20. Vieth, "Ministering to Sex Offenders," 208.

21. Noting that many children were physically or sexually abused by parents or others using Scripture as justification, therapists have found this spiritual damage can be "powerfully undone when challenged using other passages from clients' religious and spiritual tradition." Walker et al., "Sacred Texts," 175.

22. In addition to a poor understanding of speaking to children about abuse, research suggests that many Christian ministers have a poor understanding of the spiritual needs of youth in general and often base youth ministries on stereotypes as opposed to actual facts. Smith, *Soul Searching,* 266.

23. Vieth, "Augustine, Luther and Solomon," 25–33.

some segments of the church, keeping our tongue risks offending Jesus Christ (Matt 18:6–9; Luke 17:1–2; Mark 9:42).

Seventh, every church within the reach of families impacted by child abuse should implement one or more ministries to assist the hurting. As one example, the federal government has recognized as a promising practice coalitions of churches and synagogues who band together in addressing the needs of abused or neglected children when the government is unable to do so.[24]

If it is true that one out of four women and one out of six men were sexually abused as children, that more than one out of four adults were beaten as children, and one out of ten were neglected,[25] what do these numbers mean for the church? If 20 percent of our congregation had cancer or lost their home in a natural disaster, the church would no doubt respond to the needs of these parishioners immediately and with excellence.[26] The church should respond with similar compassion to maltreated children and adult survivors of abuse.

Eighth, every church should have resources for families impacted by abuse. This includes books in the church library[27] and links to *appropriate* counseling in which a licensed clinician is able to provide evidence-based therapy and, within that setting, to also address the spiritual impact of child maltreatment.[28]

Ninth, the church must answer the call to work with child protection professionals in meeting the spiritual needs of maltreated children. In a recent study of forensic interviewers who had

24. The Halos Strategy: Community Collaborations for Children, Office of Victims of Crime, https://www.ovc.gov/halos/.

25. Felitti and Anda, "Relationship of Adverse Childhood Experiences," 78–79.

26. This example was provided to the author in an e-mail from Basyle "Boz" Tchividjian, the executive director of GRACE (Godly Response to Abuse in the Christian Environment) following his review of an early draft of the paper.

27. E.g., Langberg, *Suffering and the Heart of God.*

28. The American Psychological Association has published two treatises to assist clinicians in addressing the spiritual impact of child abuse. Walker and Hathaway, *Spiritual Interventions*; Walker et al., *Spiritually Oriented Psychotherapy.*

worked with thousands of abused children, researchers found that pastors and other called workers can play a vital role in answering the spiritual questions of maltreated children.[29] The church should seize this opportunity by rigorously training and then assigning clergy to assist these children with their spiritual needs.[30]

Tenth, in all that we say and do, it must be clearly communicated to the world that we believe our treatment of children reflects our view of God. When writing a church policy on child maltreatment, for example, the preamble must remind readers that these policies are not being done to avoid litigation or reduce our insurance rate—but because children are Christ's representatives (Mark 9:36–37) and we intend to treat them with the respect due messengers of God.

---

29. Tishelman and Fontes, "Religion in Child Sexual Abuse," 120.

30. As one model for providing spiritual care, see generally, Day et al., *Risking Connection in Faith Communities.*

11

Conclusion

The Light of the World

IN HIS BOOK *VANISHING Grace*, Philip Yancey writes:

> The cross upset the long-standing categories of weak
> victims and strong heroes, for at that moment the victim
> emerged as the hero. The gospel put in motion some-
> thing new in history, which [Gil] Bailie calls "the most
> astonishing reversal of values in human history." Wher-
> ever Christianity took root, care for victims spread.[1]

As we have seen, this was certainly the case in the early
church as Christians responded to Christ's words and actions
toward children by vigorously defending them against abuse. Unfortunately, the modern church has often lost sight of abused and
neglected children—a fact attested to not only by multiple child
abuse scandals but through the scarcity of seminary training on
child abuse, through weak or nonexistent church child protection
policies, and the absence of ministries to maltreated children. This
has led more than one survivor of child abuse to ask, "How can

---

1. Yancey, *Vanishing Grace*, 170–71.

Christians worship a God who was a victim of abuse and forget to care for the victims sitting in their pews?"[2]

If this analysis is correct, it begs the question of why the contemporary church is so far behind the spirit and actions of the early church in speaking out about child maltreatment or in taking concrete actions to protect children from abuse or neglect? This difference is particularly compelling when we remember the early church did not have access to modern-day research on child maltreatment and was not being forced to act by lawsuits and bad press.

It may be the primary difference is the early church understood Jesus' words as a harsh condemnation of child abuse and acted accordingly. In contrast, the contemporary church has often forgotten, ignored, or interpreted the words of Jesus to mean something entirely different than protecting children from abuse.

It does not, of course, have to be this way. If Christians return to the scriptural accounts of Jesus and the children, the new church that arises will transform our congregations and our communities by transforming our view of children. We will at last see them as representatives of God and, as we welcome these children, we will also be welcoming Christ (Mark 9:36–37).

2. Vieth, "When God Was a Victim."

Bibliography

Albrecht, Jerome G., and Michael J. Albrecht. *Matthew*. St. Louis: Concordia, 1996.

All God's Children. Documentary. Directed by Scott Sollary and Luci Westphal. Brooklyn: Good Hard Working People, 2008.

American Academy of Pediatrics. "Guidance for Effective Discipline." *Pediatrics* 101 (1998) 723–28.

Associated Press. "Data Shed Light on Child Sexual Abuse by Protestant Clergy." *New York Times*, June 17, 2007. https://www.nytimes.com/2007/06/16/us/16protestant.html?_r=1&.

Bakke, O. M. *When Children Became People: The Birth of Childhood in Early Christianity*. Minneapolis: Augsburg Fortress, 2005.

Bartchy, Scott S. "Slaves and Slavery in the Roman World." In *The World of the New Testament: Cultural, Social, and Historical Contexts*, edited by Joel B. Green and Lee Martin McDonald, 169–78. Grand Rapids: Baker Academic, 2013.

Betsworth, Sharon. *Children in Early Christian Narratives*. London: Bloomsbury, 2015.

Betz, Janine. "Analysis of Child Abuse Training at Accredited Seminaries." Unpublished research. Gundersen National Child Protection Training Center, 2015.

Carroll, John T. "What Then Will This Child Become? Perspectives on Children in the Gospel of Luke." In *The Child in the Bible*, edited by Marcia J. Bunge, 177–94. Grand Rapids: Eerdmans, 2008.

The Catholic Teen Bible. Edited by Amy Welborn. Wichita, KS: Devore, 2011.

Child Welfare Information Gateway. "Clergy as Mandated Reporters." 2016. https://www.childwelfare.gov/pubPDFs/clergymandated.pdf.

Christianity Today. "Thou Shall Not Abuse: Reconsidering Spanking." Editorial. January 16, 2012. http://www.christianitytoday.com/ct/2012/january/editorial-spanking-abuse.html.

Cohick, Lynn H. "Women, Children and Families in the Greco-Roman World." In *The World of the New Testament: Cultural, Social, and Historical*

Contexts, edited by Joel B. Green and Lee Martin McDonald, 179–87. Grand Rapids: Baker Academic 2013.

D'Antonio, Michael. *Mortal Sins: Sex, Crime and the Era of Catholic Scandal.* New York: Dunne, 2013.

Davidson, Richard M. "Sexual Abuse in the Old Testament." In *The Long Journey Home: Understanding and Ministering to the Sexually Abused,* edited by Andrew J. Schmuzter, 136–54. Eugene, OR: Wipf & Stock, 2011.

Day, Jackson H. *Risking Connection in Faith Communities: A Training Curriculum for Faith Leaders Supporting Trauma Survivors.* Baltimore: Sidran Institute Press, 2006.

DeMause, Lloyd. *The History of Childhood.* New York: Bedrick, 1988.

Dobson, James C. *The New Dare to Discipline.* Tyndale Momentum, 2014.

Drebing, Charles, et al. "The Long Term Impact of Child Abuse on Religious Behavior and Spirituality in Men." *Child Abuse & Neglect* 22 (1998) 369–80.

Engelbrecht, Edward A., ed. *The Apocrypha: The Lutheran Edition with Notes.* St. Louis: Concordia, 2012.

Enten, Harry. "Americans' Opinions on Spanking Vary by Party, Race, Region and Religion." *FiveThirtyEight*, September 14, 2014. https://fivethirtyeight.com/datalab/americans-opinions-on-spanking-vary-by-party-race-region-and-religion/.

Evans Grubbs, Judith. "Hidden in Plain Sight." In *Children, Memory, and Family Identity in Roman Culture*, edited by Veronique Dasen and Thomas Spath, 293–310. New York: Oxford University Press, 2010.

Felitti, Vincent J., and Robert F. Anda. "The Relationship of Adverse Childhood Experiences to Adult Medical Disease, Psychiatric Disorders and Sexual Behavior: Implications for Healthcare." In *The Impact of Early Life Trauma on Health and Disease: The Hidden Epidemic*, edited by Ruth A. Lanius et al., 77–87. Cambridge: Cambridge University Press, 2010.

Finkelhor, David. "Prevention of Sexual Abuse through Educational Programs Directed toward Children." *Pediatrics* 120 (2007) 640–45.

Finkelhor, David, et al. "Poly-victimization: A Neglected Component in Child Victimization." *Journal of Child Abuse & Neglect* 31 (2007) 7–26.

Frawley-Odea, Gail Mary. "God Images in Clinical Work with Sexual Abuse Survivors: A Relational Psychodynamic Paradigm." In *Spiritually-Oriented Psychotherapy for Trauma*, edited by Donald F. Walker et al., 169–88. Washington, DC: American Psychological Association, 2015.

Gershoff, Elizabeth T. *Report on Physical Punishment in the United States: What Research Tells Us about Its Effects on Children.* Developed in conjunction with Phoenix Children's Hospital. 2008. http://www.phoenixchildrens.org/community/injury-prevention-center/effective-discipline#The_Report_on_Physical_Punishment.

Gershoff, Elizabeth T., and Andrew Grogran-Kaylor. "Spanking and Child Outcomes: Old Controversies and New Meta-Analysis." *Journal of Family Psychology* 30 (2016) 453–69.

GRACE. *Final Report for the Investigatory Review of Child Abuse at New Tribes FandaMissionary School*. August 23, 2010. http://www.akha.org/content/missiondocuments/grace-final-report-on-ntm-fanda.pdf.

———. "Startling News within the Protestant Church." Unpublished, undated manuscript.

Gundry, Judith M. "Children in the Gospel of Mark, with Special Attention to Jesus' Blessing of the Children (Mark 10:13–16) and the Purpose of the Child." In *The Child in the Bible*, edited by Marcia J. Bunge, 29–60. Grand Rapids: Eerdmans, 2008.

Gundry-Volf, Judith M. "The Least and the Greatest: Children in the New Testament." In *The Child in Christian Thought*, edited by Marcia J. Bunge, 29–60. Grand Rapids: Eerdmans, 2001.

Hinsdale, Mary Ann. "'Infinite Openness to the Infinite': Karl Rahner's Contribution to Modern Catholic Thought on the Child." In *The Child in Christian Thought*, edited by Marcia J. Bunge, 406–45. Grand Rapids: Eerdmans, 2001.

Concordia Self-Study Bible. Edited by Robert G. Hoerber. St. Louis: Concordia, 1986.

Hoffman, John P., et al. "Conservative Protestantism and Attitudes toward Corporal Punishment." *Social Science Research* 63 (2017) 81–94.

Joersz, Jerald C. *Galatians, Ephesians & Philippians*. St. Louis: Concordia, 2013.

John Jay College of Criminal Justice. "The Nature and Scope of Sexual Abuse of Minors by Catholic Priests and Deacons in the United States 1950–2002." February 2004.

Joyce, Kathryn. "By Grace Alone." *American Prospect*, May 4, 2014. http://prospect.org/article/next-christian-sex-abuse-scandal.

Knox, Barbara L., et al. "Child Torture as a form of Child Abuse." *Journal of Child and Adolescent Trauma* 7 (2014) 37–49.

Kolb, Robert, and Timothy J. Wengert, eds. *The Book of Concord: The Confessions of the Evangelical Lutheran Church*. Minneapolis: Fortress, 2000.

Laes, Christian. *Children in the Roman Empire*. New York: Cambridge University Press, 2011.

Langberg, Diane. *Suffering and the Heart of God: How Trauma Destroys and Christ Restores*. Greensboro, NC: New Growth, 2015.

Loader, William. *Making Sense of Sex: Attitudes Towards Sexuality in Early Jewish and Christian Literature*. Grand Rapids: Eerdmans, 2013.

———. *The New Testament on Sexuality*. Grand Rapids: Eerdmans, 2012.

Luther, Martin. *Annotations on Matthew: Chapters 1–18*. Edited by Jaroslav Pelikan and Helmut T. Lehmann. American ed. Luther's Works 67. Philadelphia: Fortress, 1965.

Lytton, Timothy D. *Holding Bishops Accountable: How Lawsuits Helped the Catholic Church Confront Sexual Abuse*. Cambridge: Harvard University Press, 2008.

MacDonald, Margaret Y. *The Power of Children*. Waco: Baylor University Press, 2014.

Marcus, Joel. *Mark 8–16*. New Haven: Yale University Press, 2009.

McLaughlin, Barbara R. "Devastated Spirituality: The Impact of Clergy Sexual Abuse on the Survivor's Relationship with God." *Sexual Addiction & Compulsivity* 1 (1994) 145–58.

Miller-Perrin, Cindy, and Robin Perrin. "Changing Attitudes about Spanking among Conservative Christians Using Interventions That Focus on Empirical Research Evidence and Progressive Biblical Interpretations." *Child Abuse & Neglect* 71 (2017) 69–79.

Mohler, Albert. "Should Spanking Be Banned? Parental Authority under Assault." AlbertMohler.com. June 22, 2004. http://www.albertmohler.com/2004/06/22/should-spanking-be-banned-parental-authority-under-assault/.

The New Annotated Oxford Bible. Edited by Michael D. Coogan. 4th ed. Oxford: Oxford University Press, 2010.

Offit, Paul A. *Bad Faith: When Religious Belief Undermines Modern Medicine*. New York: Basic, 2015.

Paavola, Daniel E. *Mark*. St. Louis: Concordia, 2013.

Payne, Gregory Henry. *The Child in Human Progress*. New York: Knickerbocker, 1916.

Pearl, Michael, and Debi Pearl. *To Train Up a Child*. Pleasantville, TN: No Greater Joy Ministries, 2015.

Pérez-Peña, Richard. "Bob Jones University Blamed Victims of Sexual Assaults, Not Abusers, Report Says." *New York Times*, December 11, 2014. https://www.nytimes.com/2014/12/12/us/bob-jones-university-sex-assault-victim-study.html?_r=0.

Perrin, Robin, et al. "Changing Attitudes about Spanking Using Alternative Biblical Interpretations." *International Journal of Behavioral Development* 41 (2017) 514–22.

Reju, Deepak. *On Guard: Preventing and Responding to Child Abuse at Church*. Greensboro, NC: New Growth, 2014.

Rueger, Matthew. *Sexual Morality in a Christless World*. St. Louis: Concordia, 2016.

Saul, Janet, and Natalie C. Audage. *Preventing Child Sexual Abuse within Youth-Serving Organizations: Getting Started on Policies and Procedures*. Washington, DC: Centers for Disease Control and Prevention, 2007.

Schuetze, John D. "Pastoral Theology Brief: Matthew 18 Also Includes Verse 6." *Wisconsin Lutheran Quarterly* 112 (2015) 224–28.

Smith, Christian. *Soul Searching: The Religious and Spiritual Lives of American Teenagers*. Oxford: Oxford University Press, 2005.

Stafford, Wess. *Too Small to Ignore*. Colorado Springs: Waterbrook, 2007.

Strange, W. A. *Children in the Early Church*. Eugene, OR: Wipf and Stock, 2004.

Suelflow, August R. *Servant of the Word: The Life and Ministry of C. F. W. Walther*. St. Louis: Concordia, 2000.

Tchividjian, Basyle, and Shira M. Berkovits. *The Child Safeguarding Policy Guide for Churches and Ministries*. Greensboro, NC: New Growth, 2017.

Terry, Karen J., et al. *The Causes and Context of Sexual Abuse of Minors by Catholic Priests in the United States, 1950–2010*. Washington, DC: United States Conference of Catholic Bishops, 2011.

Tishelman, Amy C., and Lisa S. Fontes. "Religion in Child Sexual Abuse Forensic Interviews." *Child Abuse & Neglect* 63 (2017) 120–30.

Tracy, Steven R. *Mending the Soul*. Grand Rapids: Zondervan, 2005.

Turner, Heather A., et al. "Poly-victimization in a National Sample of Children and Youth." *American Journal of Preventive Medicine* 38 (2010) 323–30.

US Department of Justice. *Executive Summary: Report of the Attorney General's Task Force on Children Exposed to Violence*. Office of Juvenile Justice and Delinquency Prevention, 2012.

Vieth, Victor I. "Augustine, Luther and Solomon: Providing Pastoral Guidance to Parents on the Corporal Punishment of Children." *Currents in Mission & Theology* 44 (2017) 25–33.

———. "Keeping the Faith: A Call for Collaboration between the Faith and Child Protection Communities." In *Medical, Legal & Social Science Aspects of Child Sexual Exploitation*, edited by Sharon W. Cooper, 947–64. St. Louis: GW Medical Publishing, 2005.

———. "Ministering to Sex Offenders: Ten Lessons from Henry Gerecke." *Wisconsin Lutheran Quarterly* 112 (2015) 208–23.

———. "Suffer the Children: Developing Effective Church Policies on Child Maltreatment." *Jacob's Hope* 2 (2011) 1–8.

———. "Ten Things the Church Can Do to Help Abused Children." *Persistent Voice*. May 2, 2016. https://thepersistentvoice.wordpress.com/2016/05/.

———. "What Would Walther Do? Applying Law & Gospel to Victims and Perpetrators of Child Sexual Abuse." *Journal of Psychology & Theology* 40 (2012) 257–73.

———. "When God Was a Victim: What a Child Abuse Survivor Taught Me about Good Friday." *Religion News Service*, April 2, 2015. http://religionnews.com/2015/04/02/god-victim-child-abuse-survivor-taught-good-friday/.

———. "When Is It Safe to Go Back to Church?" *Boundless*. October 13, 2014. http://www.boundless.org/relationships/2014/is-it-safe-to-go-back-to-church.

Walker, Donald F., and William L. Hathaway, eds. *Spiritual Interventions in Child and Adolescent Psychotherapy*. Washington, DC: American Psychological Association, 2013.

Walker, Donald F., et al. "Changes in Personal Religion/Spirituality During and After Childhood Abuse: A Review and Synthesis." *Psychological Trauma: Theory, Research, Practice, and Policy* 1 (2009) 130–45.

Walker, Donald F., et al. "Sacred Texts." In *Spiritual Interventions in Child and Adolescent Therapy*, edited by Donald F. Walker and William L. Hathaway, 155–80. Washington, DC: American Psychological Association, 2013.

Walker, Donald F., et al. *Spiritually Oriented Psychotherapy for Trauma*. Washington, DC: American Psychological Association, 2015.

Walther, C. F. W. *God Grant It.* St. Louis: Concordia, 2006.

Watson, Terri S. "Counseling the Abuse Victim: Integrating Evidence-Based Practice Guidelines with Spiritual Resources." In *The Long Journey Home: Understanding and Ministering to the Sexually Abused,* edited by Andrew J. Schmuzter, 248–61. Eugene, OR: Wipf & Stock, 2011.

Webb, William J. *Corporal Punishment in the Bible.* Downers Grove: InterVarsity, 2011.

Wengert, Timothy J. *Martin Luther's Catechisms: Forming the Faith.* Minneapolis: Fortress, 2009.

White, Keith J. "'He Placed a Little Child in the Midst': Jesus, the Kingdom, and Children." In *The Child in the Bible,* edited by Marcia J. Bunge, 353–74. Grand Rapids: Eerdmans, 2008.

World Council of Churches (WCC). *Confessing the One Faith: An Ecumenical Explication of the Apostolic Faith as It Is Confessed in the Nicene-Constantinopolitan Creed.* Eugene, OR: Wipf and Stock, 2010.

Wurtele, Sandy K., and Maureen C. Kenny. "Primary Prevention of Child Sexual Abuse: Child and Parent Focused Approaches." In *The Prevention of Sexual Violence: A Practitioner's Sourcebook,* edited by Keith L. Kaufman, 107–20. Holyoke, MA: Neari, 2010.

Yancey, Phillip. *Vanishing Grace.* Grand Rapids: Zondervan, 2014.

Yarbro Collins, Adela. *Mark: A Commentary.* Minneapolis: Fortress, 2007.

Yinger, Kent L. "Jewish Education." In *The World of the New Testament: Cultural, Social, and Historical Contexts,* edited by Joel B. Green and Lee Martin McDonald, 325–29. Grand Rapids: Baker Academic, 2013.

Zylstra, Sarah Eekhoff. "Missionary Donn Ketcham Abused 18 Children: Here's Why He Wasn't Stopped." *Christianity Today,* May 10, 2016. http://www.christianitytoday.com/ct/2016/may-web-only/missionary-donn-ketcham-abuse-bangladesh-mks-abwe-report.html.

19953400R00046

Made in the USA
Middletown, DE
08 December 2018